Program Authors

Lindamichelle Baron • Sharon Sicinski-Skeans

Modern Curriculum Press

Parsippany, New Jersey

Special thanks to the following schools for providing student writing samples:

Allendale Elementary School
Oakland, CA

Camden Elementary School, Camden, NJ

Center Ridge Elementary School
Centreville, VA

Chattanooga School for Arts and Science
Chattanooga, TN

Clinton Elementary School, Maplewood, NJ

Crown Community Academy, Chicago, IL

Glenwood Elementary, Short Hills, NJ

Jackson School, Des Moines, IA

Kennedy Elementary School, Santa Ana, CA

Steelton-Highspire Elementary School
Steelton, PA

Wadsworth Elementary School
Chicago, IL

Weslaco ISD
Weslaco, TX

William Halley Elementary School
Fairfax Station, VA

Project Editor: *Judy Giglio* • **Designers:** *Lisa Arcuri, Terry Taylor, Dorothea Fox & Sue Ligertwood*
Cover Design: *Senja Lauderdale & Chris Otazo* • **Cover Illustration:** *Bernard Adnet*

Acknowledgments

Amber Brown Goes Fourth by Paula Danziger. Illustrated by Tony Ross. Text copyright © 1995 by Paula Danziger. Illustrations copyright © 1995 by Tony Ross. Reprinted by permission of G.P. Putnam's Sons, a division of The Putnam & Grosset Group.

"Bookworm" from *Go With the Poem* by Mary Ann Hoberman. Copyright © 1975 by Mary Ann Hoberman. Reprinted by permission of Gina Maccoby Literary Agency.

"Charlotte's Web (Dramatization)" by Joseph Robinette from *Plays Children Love, Volume II* edited by Coleman A. Jennings and Aurand Harris. Text copyright © 1983 by Dramatic Publishing Company. Reprinted by permission of Dramatic Publishing Company and St. Martin Press.

"Down Into the Blue Sea" from *Dolphin Adventure* by Wayne Grover. Illustrated by Jim Fowler. Text copyright © 1990 by Wayne Grover. Illustrations copyright © 1990 by Jim Fowler. Reprinted by permission of Greenwillow Books, a division of William Morrow & Company, Inc.

"Hey, It Doesn't Work" by Kathleen M. Kowalski from *Girls' Life* magazine. Reprinted by permission of *Girls' Life* magazine.

"Please Bird" from *Flower Moon Snow: A Book of Haiku* by Kazue Mizumura. Copyright © 1977 by Kazue Mizumura. Used by permission of HarperCollins Publishers.

"Space Camp Brochure" U.S. SPACE CAMP ®, U.S. SPACE ACADEMY ®, SPACE CAMP ®, SPACE ACADEMY ®, ADVANCED SPACE ACADEMY ™, AVIATION CHALLENGE ®, and SPACE GEAR ® are registered trademarks and service marks of the U.S. Space & Rocket Center. The UNITED STATES ASTRONAUT HALL OF FAME ® is a registered trademark of the U.S. Space Camp Foundation. All rights reserved. Entire contents copyrighted © 1997 Alabama Space Science Exhibit Commission. No reproduction of photographs permitted without written permission. Reprinted by permission of U.S. Space Camp Foundation.

"The Stray" reprinted with the permission of Simon & Schuster Books for Young Readers, an imprint of Simon & Schuster Children's Publishing Division from *Every Living Thing* by Cynthia Rylant, illustrated by S.D. Schindler. Copyright © 1985 Cynthia Rylant. Jacket illustration by S.D. Schindler. Copyright © 1985 Simon & Schuster.

"Dictionary entry" from *Webster's New World Dictionary for Explorers of Language.* Copyright © 1991 by Simon & Schuster. Reprinted with permission of Modern Curriculum Press.

Art and photo credits appear on page 282.

Modern Curriculum Press

An Imprint of Pearson Learning
299 Jefferson Road, P.O. Box 480 • Parsippany, NJ 07054-0480
www.mcschool.com

ISBN: 0-7652-0751-6

3 4 5 6 7 8 9 10   RRD   07 06 05 04 03 02 01 00

Contents

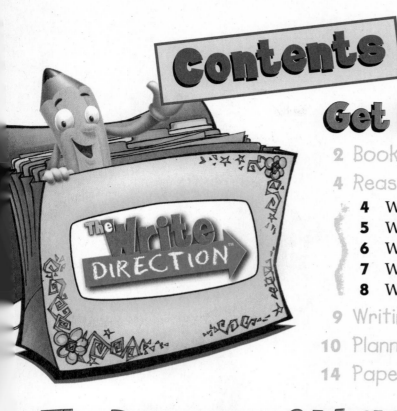

Are you going in The Write Direction?

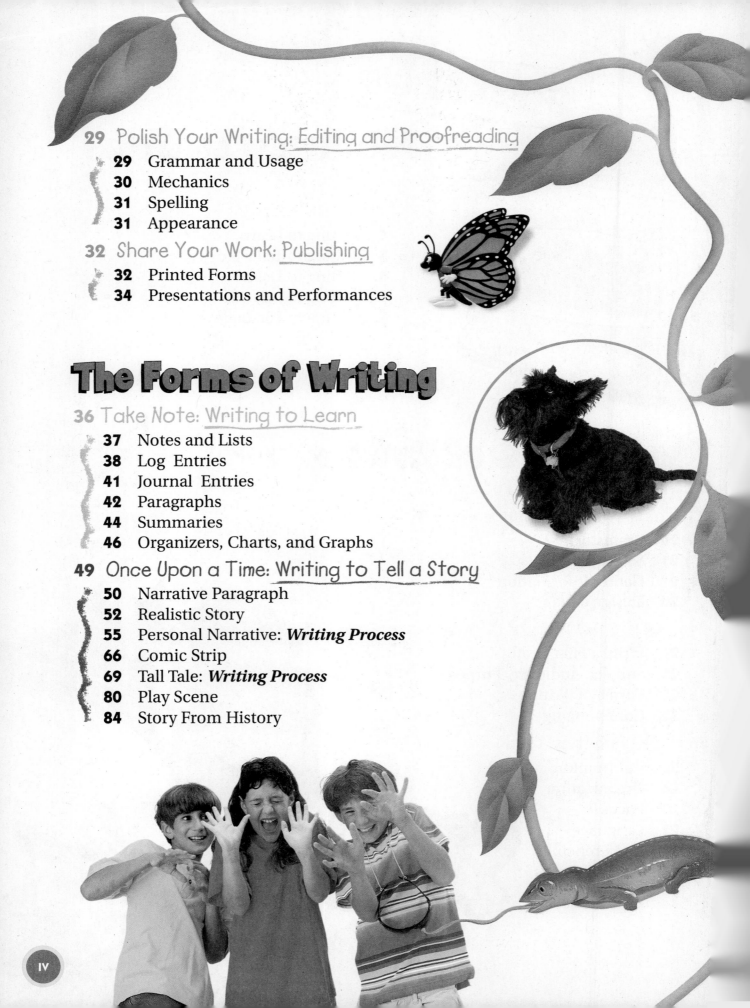

The Forms of Writing

Writer's Handbook

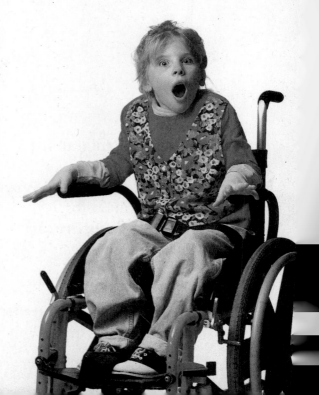

GET READY TO WRITE

Book Tour—A Quick Look

What is this book all about?

The Write Direction is a book full of explanations, models, and ideas for doing all kinds of writing. The book has four main sections or units.

This tour will get you going in **The Write Direction**.

Get Ready to Write

This first unit starts you on your way by introducing the five reasons for writing—to learn, to tell a story, to describe, to inform, and to persuade.

The Process of Writing

This unit takes you through the writing stages that all successful writers follow when they write. These stages are prewriting, drafting, revising, editing and proofreading, and publishing.

The Forms of Writing

Once you learn about the many forms of writing in this unit, you'll be able to write your own stories, poems, reports, letters, plays, and more.

Writer's Handbook

This section helps you become a Super Writer! The first part, Writer's Craft, explains terms that every writer needs to know. The remaining part provides tips about grammar, punctuation, and spelling.

What are the special features in this book?

You'll find six special features throughout *The Write Direction*. Look through the book to find examples of each one.

Your Turn

Good writing doesn't just happen. You've got to write to get good at it. Your Turn gives you the chance to try out the skills you have learned.

Writer's Tip
These tips suggest what an experienced writer would do. Try them and see if they work for you.

Become a Super Writer

These suggestions lead you to helpful lessons about writing or language skills.

Think Like a Writer ★ These questions help you connect what you've just learned to your own writing.

Tech Tip

These are hints for working on a computer. Soon you'll be keyboarding with the pros.

Portfolio

This is a reminder to save your writing in an organized way. A portfolio shows how far you have come as a writer.

How can you get to know your book?

Look through *The Write Direction*. Check out a lesson or the handbook. Take a peek at models written by students and professionals. Then just for fun, use the table of contents and index to find answers to these questions.

On which pages will you find
- a published author's limerick?
- a famous comic strip?
- a really cool brochure?
- writing done by real kids?
- how to use a thesaurus?

Welcome back! You've traveled in *The Write Direction!*

Writing to Learn

You learn something new every day!

There are many different ways in which you learn. You are learning every time you

- read a book
- watch a video
- speak with another person
- listen to someone

One way to remember new information is to write it down. Writing lets you hold on to ideas so you can think about them. When your reason for writing is to plan, record, remember, organize, list, or ask questions, then you are writing to learn!

Take a look at some ideas for how to make notes. Check them out!

Think Like a Writer

★ Which subject is the hardest for you?

★ How will jotting down important ideas and examples help you learn?

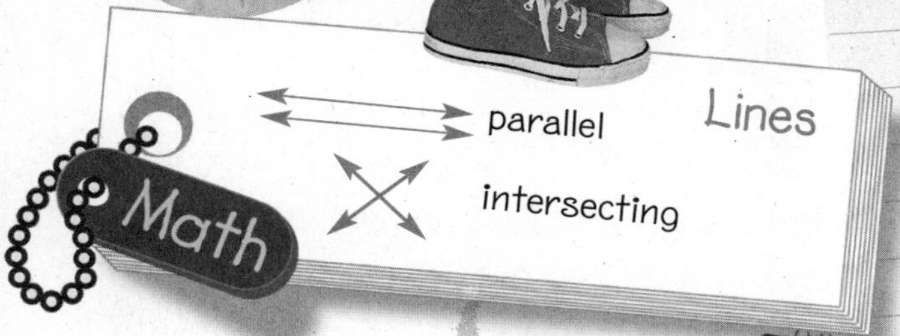

Science

Weather Words

front:
a place where two air masses meet

symbols:
warm front
cold front

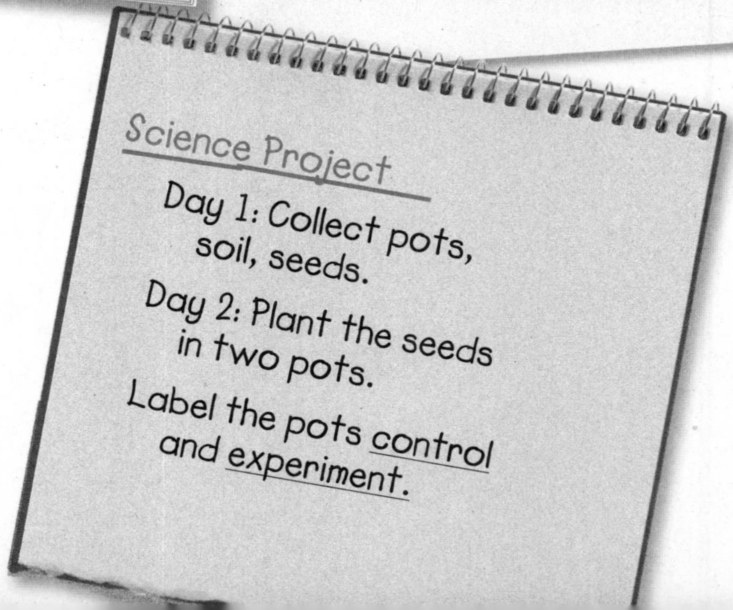

Lines

parallel

intersecting

Math

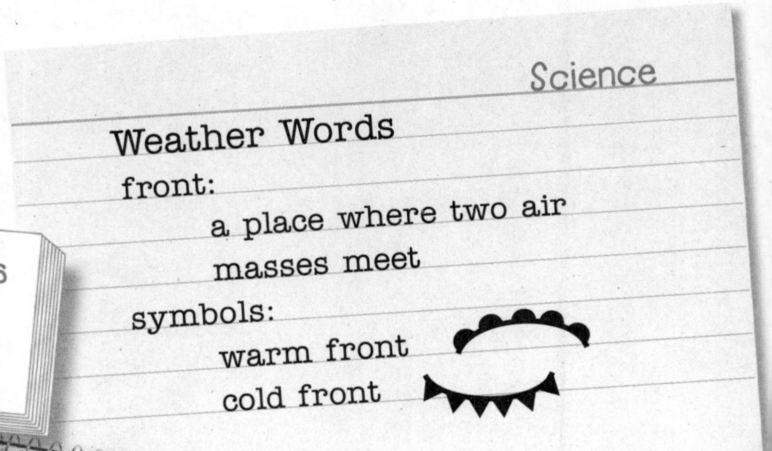

Science Project

Day 1: Collect pots, soil, seeds.

Day 2: Plant the seeds in two pots.

Label the pots <u>control</u> and <u>experiment</u>.

Writing to Tell a Story

What kinds of stories do you enjoy reading?

- an action adventure
- a story about everyday people
- a scary mystery
- a story that takes you back in time

Stories come in different forms, but all stories let the reader know who the characters are, where the story takes place, and what happens.

What do you have to remember as a storyteller?

Keep in mind that you want to write about characters and events that your readers will find interesting and entertaining. You can make your readers laugh out loud with a funny story. You can give them goose bumps with a scary tale or take them along on an awesome adventure. It's up to you. Who and what do you picture as you read these stories?

Personal Narrative

I was so excited when the first letter from my new penpal arrived in the mail. Her name is Lili, and she lives on the Big Island, Hawaii, near the active volcano Kilauea!

Play

Mac: **"This jungle sure is creepy."** *[looking overhead]*

Carla: *[pointing to the ground]* **"I hope we don't see an anaconda."**

Tall Tale

Cactus Cal lives in the deserts of Arizona. He wears leather and rides a giant rattler. He has an appetite the size of the Grand Canyon.

Think Like a Writer

★ Why is it important to know what kinds of stories your readers enjoy the most?

★ How can you keep them interested as they read?

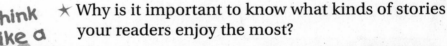

Writing to Describe

How is a writer an artist?

If you want to describe what a certain person, place, or thing is like, you could share a photograph, a sketch, or a home video. You could also "paint a picture" with words.

Whether your subject is real or imagined, your purpose is to give specific details to tell what your subject is like in a way that makes it real to your readers.

How can words help your readers see what you see?

When you write to describe, choose vivid words to help your readers see, feel, smell, taste, or hear. Just one or two "right" words can make the difference between a boring description and a perfect picture. How do these writers use language to help you see and feel what's happening?

> The intruder was six feet tall with ears and legs like a jack rabbit. However, a long brown tail was sticking out from under his overcoat. Is my suspect really a kangaroo?
>
> Mystery Story

> I rode on my first roller coaster today. Going up, the ride was smooth. Then we bounced over the top of the first hill and started down. My stomach was in my throat. I was dizzy with happiness. I couldn't wait until the next hill.
>
> Paragraph

Think Like a Writer

★ What kind of description would you enjoy writing? Why?

★ How can you make your readers feel as if they are seeing the same thing you see?

Writing to Inform

What subjects capture your attention?

- a favorite team in sports
- current fads
- how to do or make things
- famous people in the news

When you write to give readers facts about subjects that interest you, you are writing to inform.

As a writer, what real-life topics could you inform readers about?

Subjects that interest you probably will interest your readers, too. Your topic can be something you already know a lot about. It can also be something that has just caught your attention and makes you curious. How does each of these writers share information?

Dear Pat,

I asked around about summer jobs for kids our age. Some kids wash cars or take care of pets. Some do garden work. My best friend works in her mother's home office. What good jobs have you heard about?

Your friend,

Chris

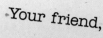

Letter

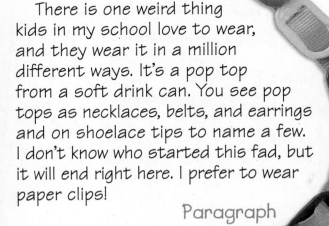

There is one weird thing kids in my school love to wear, and they wear it in a million different ways. It's a pop top from a soft drink can. You see pop tops as necklaces, belts, and earrings and on shoelace tips to name a few. I don't know who started this fad, but it will end right here. I prefer to wear paper clips!

Paragraph

Think Like a Writer

★ What information could you share with an audience?

★ How could you make it interesting to more readers?

Writing to Persuade

When do you want your opinion heard?

- You'd like a raise in your allowance.
- You want to convince the town to install brighter street lights near school.
- You need to encourage people to volunteer for some school activity.

When you feel strongly about a topic and convince other people to agree with you, you are persuading them. You hope the reasons you give will move them to act.

How can you get your readers to agree with you?

When you state your opinion about a subject and offer good reasons for it, you are writing to persuade. Choose reasons that will convince your readers. These are the people whose opinions you are trying to change. Why are these pieces of writing persuasive?

Hey, everybody!

Don't forget to sign up for

indoor rock climbing.

- It's great exercise.
- Instructors show you how to climb safely.
- Safety ropes hold you up.

✍ Sign up today!

Poster

Vote for me to be Science Club president. I read a lot of science books, and I like to do experiments. I even spent two weeks at a space camp. If you pick me, I'll make the club feel proud!

Speech

Think Like a Writer
★ What topics do you feel strongly about?
★ How can you get your readers to agree with you?

Writing for Yourself and Others

When is writing personal?

Writing is not always meant to be read by others. Sometimes you write just for yourself.

- study notes
- an entry in your journal or diary
- things-to-do lists and schedules
- literature and observation logs

When do you write for others?

Some writing is for your teacher or for others to read.

- book reports and research reports
- stories, articles, and poems
- notes or postcards to friends

What reason did each of these students have for writing?

Saturday–May 26

Last night I dreamed that I was surrounded by giant cones that were dripping all over me. I was caught in a river of melted yogurt when I woke up. No more yogurt before bed for me!

Journal

An Interview With Aunt Serena

My Aunt Serena is a registered nurse. She worked in a dress store for a year until she realized she really wanted to help sick people. So she quit her job and went to nursing school. Today she is an operating room nurse at Quincy Memorial Hospital. She is studying to become a nurse practitioner.

Character Sketch

Think Like a Writer
- ★ What things do you write just for yourself?
- ★ How do you feel about sharing your writing with an audience?

Planning Your Portfolio

Get organized as a writer!

As you write more often, your writing will get better. The best way to see how much you have improved is to save your writing in an organized way. This is your writing portfolio.

Portfolio

It is time to use your portfolio when you see this logo.

What's a Portfolio?

A portfolio is a collection of your work that can be kept in a folder, a binder, or some other special place. Throughout this book you'll see a portfolio logo. It will remind you when and where to save your writing.

A portfolio shows your work and growth as a writer. You'll be able to set goals for skills you need to work on. Most of all you'll have a collection of writing pieces that tells you and others that you're a writer.

A Portfolio Model

Most of your writing is done over a period of time. From prewriting to your final copy, you collect a stack of paper. You may have charts, diagrams, notes, and sketches. It's easy to misplace something important. Your portfolio helps you keep things together.

Every time you start a new piece of writing, clip the following things together.

- prewriting and brainstorming notes
- first draft with revising marks
- pictures, drawings, charts that go along with the writing
- your final copy

This writer stores her prewriting notes and draft in her portfolio under a section labeled "Work in Progress." When she has a final copy, she will move it to a section labeled "Finished Pieces."

I use a large paper clip to hold my notes and first draft together.

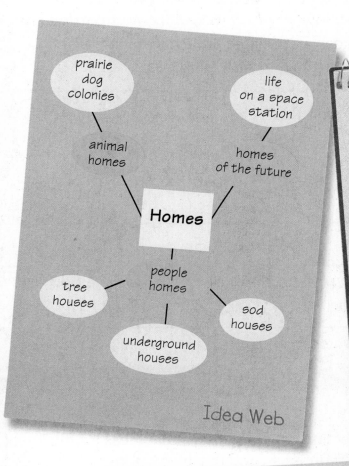

Idea Web

Unusual Homes for People Today

1. TREE HOUSE
   - Maine, Vermont
   - many rooms in big trees with electricity

2. SOD HOUSE
   - Montana
   - earth-sheltered house looks like a cave with windows

3. UNDERGROUND HOUSE
   - New Jersey

Notes

I was looking through some magazines. I saw photographs of tree houses. Also, I saw people living in caves. I couldn't believe it. Can you? The first picture shows a tree house in Maine.

Draft

How can you make a portfolio?

If you do a lot of writing in your class, your teacher may suggest the best way to set up a portfolio. Here are some suggestions.

Getting Started

Choose a large pocket folder, a roomy envelope, or even a ring binder to hold all your pieces of writing. Clearly label it with your name and decorate it in your own style.

Organization

- Your portfolio won't do you much good if you can't find what's in it. Decide how you will organize your portfolio.

- One idea is to keep an updated table of contents or schedule for yourself.

My Table of Contents

Title	Prewriting Date	Publishing Date
Pigs for Pets	Sept. 5	Sept. 6
Book Report on Shiloh by Phyllis Naylor	Sept. 8	Sept. 12
Unusual Homes	Sept. 15	

- You can have sections for word lists, great ideas for future writing, works in progress, and finished writing.

- You might decide to organize your portfolio according to different kinds of writing. Colorful partitions or tabs are good to use to separate these sections.

Storage

- Store your portfolio along with those of your classmates. Use the special place in the classroom your teacher has set aside.
- Always remember to return your portfolio to its proper place at the end of the period.

Portfolio Evaluation

Some portfolios have a special purpose. Your teacher may ask you to keep a special "showcase" portfolio in addition to your regular "working" portfolio. In your showcase portfolio, you keep your best work. Your teacher will use this portfolio at the end of a grading period to check the progress you've made as a writer.

Set up your own portfolio. Choose and prepare a folder or binder to collect your work. Use tabs or partitions to organize your portfolio sections. Make your portfolio special by the way you organize it. Put together a portfolio that will represent your work and talent as a writer.

Writer's Tip
If you want to take home some samples of your work, ask your teacher to make copies so that one stays in your portfolio.

Paper, Pen, and Word Processing

> I use my best handwriting for my final draft.

How can you make your writing look good?

Here are some ways to make your writing easy to work on and easy to read.

For Your First Draft

- Use lined yellow paper to show it's a work in progress.
- Write on every other line so that you have space to make changes.
- Write on one side of the paper only so that you can cut and paste.

Keep Away

Try a game called <u>Keep Away</u>.

One thing about this game is that you need a lot of friends to play. The only thing you need is a soccer ball. Two teams try to keep the ball by passing it.

A Friendly Game

If you are looking for a great game to play with friends, try a game called <u>Keep Away</u>. The first great thing about this game is that you need a lot of friends to play. The only equipment you need is a soccer ball. Members from two teams try to keep the ball by passing it to teammates. Each pass earns one point. The team with the most number of passes is the winner. The first rule for playing is to have fun!

For Your Final Copy

- Use lined white paper to show it's your final draft.
- Start on the top line. Leave a margin of one inch on both sides and the bottom.
- Use your best handwriting. Print or use cursive script as your teacher directs.
- Be neat. If the paper starts to look sloppy, start a new, clean copy.

Think Like a Writer ★ Why is a neat and readable draft important to a writer?

Here are some tips for writing on a computer.

Unless there's a computer for everyone in your classroom, you probably do your planning and first draft by hand. Then you type your draft on the computer.

File   Edit   View   Label   Special

Naming your file
Pick a good name for your file. *Fish* is a better name for a report about fish than *Report*.

Saving your file
Learn how your program saves files. Save often as you work. Always save your file before you exit, or quit, the program.

Typing your file
Learn where the keys are. Use special keys like Backspace and Delete. Practice using the cursor keys and the mouse or trackball.

Editing your file
Use the icons or the File and Edit menus to see how to delete a word, a line, or a paragraph and how to cut and paste.

Checking the spelling
Most word-processing programs let you check your spelling.

Printing your file
Click on the icon or the word *Print* from the File menu. Always save and print a copy of your work before you exit.

Think Like a Writer

★ In what ways will using a computer make revising, editing, and proofreading easier?

Computer Keyboard

THE PROCESS OF WRITING

The Stages in the Process

Writing is not just moving a pen or pencil across a sheet of paper. Writing involves thinking, planning, and gathering thoughts and facts. It often means changing what you have already written. This is why writing is called a process.

Many writers find it helpful to follow certain steps as they write. These steps are the stages of the writing process.

1. Prewriting

The purpose of this first stage is to get ready to write. It is the time for exploring ideas.

- Brainstorm and get ideas.
- Select a topic.
- Gather information.
- Design a plan.

5. Publishing

If you want to make your writing public, now is the time. You choose the way to publish that works best for you.

- Send a letter or an E-mail.
- Make a book.
- Tell a story.
- Put on a play.

2. Drafting

This stage is all about getting your words on paper so you can look over what you have written and think about it some more.

- Write freely.
- Let your plan be your guide.

Writer's Tip
Remember, at any time you can go back and repeat a stage of the writing process.

3. Revising

This is your chance to make a few or a lot of changes. Decide how you will improve your writing.

- Read your draft.
- Share it with a partner.
- Move, add, and take out words.

4. Editing and Proofreading

It's important to check your writing so that it reads smoothly. During this stage you make sure every detail is correct.

- Check grammar, capitalization, punctuation, and spelling.
- Make a clean copy.
- Proofread one last time.

Prewriting

Think It Through

Prewriting is the first stage in the process of writing. During this stage a writer gets ready to write by thinking, making choices, gathering information, planning, and sharing. Good writers don't begin to write before they have made a plan. A plan helps you know where you are going.

camping
observing butterflies
picking blueberries
my first sleepover
winning soccer team
moving day

A plan keeps you organized and reminds you of your

subject: What am I writing about?

audience: Who will read what I write?

purpose: Why am I writing this?

form: How will I write about my subject?

Brainstorm

When you brainstorm, you think of as many ideas as you can. Often one idea leads to another, and before you know it, you've found a topic you want to write about.

Brainstorm by writing down all your ideas on paper.

- Make a list of experiences and events in your life.
- Do a quick write. Choose a subject and write down everything you know about it. Don't stop until you run out of ideas.

Brainstorm by talking with others.

- Share memories with friends.
- Exchange ideas you got from reading.

Think Like a Writer
★ How will brainstorming help you think of ideas you didn't know you had?

Select a Topic

Look over the ideas you have written down. Think about the ideas you have shared. Choose the one that is most important to you.

Decide how much to say about your topic. You can't say everything. If your topic is too big, choose one part of it to write about.

When you think you're ready to begin writing, take a minute to finish this sentence. It will remind you about your subject, audience, purpose, and form.

I am writing this report about monarch butterflies for my classmates to read because I want them to learn about how these butterflies migrate.

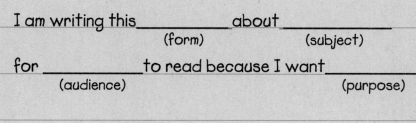

I am writing this_____ about _____
                    (form)   (subject)

for _____ to read because I want_____.
     (audience)   (purpose)

Gather Information

Once you have a great idea for writing, it's time to gather information.

- Begin by writing down questions about your topic. If you already did a quick write, you can use it to answer the questions you know.

- Find answers to the questions you don't know by reading, by asking someone, or by observing and taking notes.

- Make a chart to collect and organize your information. Here are some examples.

Detail · Detail · Topic · Detail · Detail

Cluster

More Ways to Gather and Organize Information

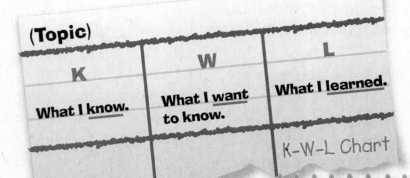

(Topic)		
K	**W**	**L**
What I know.	What I want to know.	What I learned.

K-W-L Chart

Writer's Tip
The more information you gather, the more you have to choose from when you start to write.

Favorite Butterflies

Students

30
25
20
15
10
5
0

Monarch   Tiger swallowtail   Pearly eye   Silvery blue

Types of Butterflies

Graph

Questions	(TOPIC)				
	Information from Books	Magazines	Videos	Web Sites	Interviews
1.					
2.					
3.					

Gathering Chart

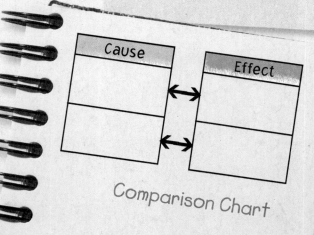

Cause	Effect

Comparison Chart

Think Like a Writer

★ Why will questions about your topic that ask *who, what, when, where,* and *how* help you? What else would your audience want to know?

Design a Plan

You have gathered and organized information about your topic. Now it is time to design a writing plan. A plan will help keep you on track. Look at your plan often as you write so that you will remember to include all important details.

A writing plan can take many forms. Choose the plan that works best for the form of writing you will be doing. Here are a few.

Beginning
(Introduce main characters, setting, and theme.)

Middle
(Tell events in a logical order.)

End
(Tell how everything works out.)

Story Map

1 → 2 → 3 → 4 → 5 → 6

Beginning   **Middle**   **End**
Time Line

Think Like a Writer

★ Why do you think certain writing plans work better with certain writing forms?

★ For what kind of writing project would you use a story map for a plan? a time line? an outline? a Venn diagram?

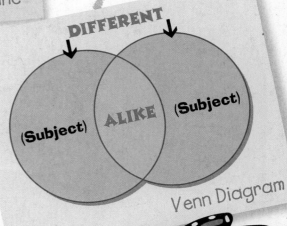

DIFFERENT

(Subject)   **ALIKE**   (Subject)

Venn Diagram

(Topic)
I. (Main Idea)
    A. (Example)
    B. (Example)
      1. (Detail)
      2. (Detail)
Outline

Drafting Put It Into Words

Once you have chosen a topic, gathered information, and designed a writing plan, the writing can begin. This is the part of the writing process called drafting.

- Drafting gets you started.
- Drafting lets you try out your ideas.
- You can change anything you want—it's only a draft!

Writing a First Draft

Start by looking at your writing plan. Take a deep breath. Then start writing. Let ideas and words flow one after another. Don't worry about grammar or spelling yet. Just write!

Writer's Tip
Skip lines when you write your first draft. That will give you room to make changes later on!

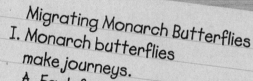

Draft #1
    Monarch butterflies are great travelers. Each fall they leave their homes in the northern United States and Canada. For parts of California, Florida, and Mexico. They make one of Earth's greatest journeys.

Migrating Monarch Butterflies
I. Monarch butterflies make journeys.
    A. Each fall they fly south.
        1. From Canada and the United States to California, Florida, and Mexico.
        2. Journey can be up to 2,000 miles (3,200 kilometers).
    B. Butterflies return home in the spring.
        1. Not all butterflies survive.
        2. New butterflies hatch during trip.

Subject, Audience, Purpose

As you write, follow your writing plan to stick to your **subject.** Think about your **audience.** Decide what your readers need to know or would enjoy learning.

Think Like a Writer

★ Would you write information about butterflies for a kindergarten class in the same way you would write for your classmates?

Your **purpose** is your reason for writing. As you write, keep that purpose in mind to make sure that what you write matches your purpose. There are five purposes for writing.

Writing to learn

Writing to tell a story

Writing to inform

Writing to describe

Writing to persuade

Forms of Writing

There are many writing forms a writer can choose, such as a letter or a story, a report, or a riddle. It is very important to choose a form that matches your purpose and audience.

Conferencing

Read what you have written to a partner. Ask yourself these questions.

- Is my purpose for writing clear?
- Does my form match my purpose and audience?

Listen to your partner's suggestions to make changes and improvements in your writing.

Revising — Take Another Look

Have you ever asked for a "do over" in a game? At one time or another, most people wish they could change a move or redo something in a game.

Writing is different because you almost always get a second chance. Revising is the third stage in the writing process. It is your chance to make changes and improvements.

Information

When you revise your writing, first check the information you have used. Correct mistakes, add ideas and details, or even take out some information.

Organization

Revising is also the time to make sure you have organized your writing well. Sometimes moving a sentence will make your writing clearer.

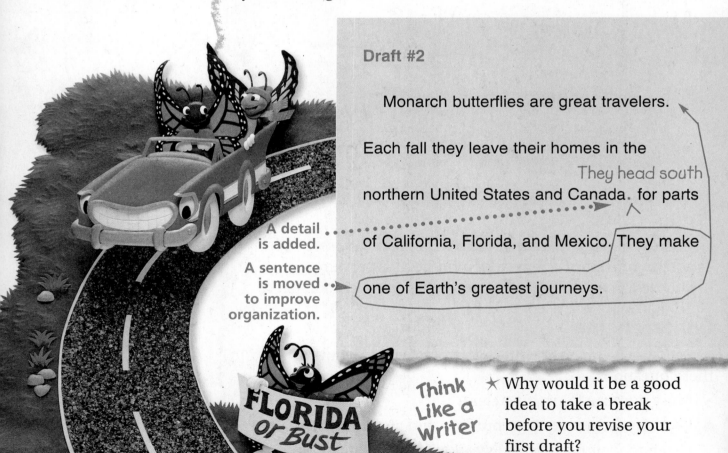

Draft #2

Monarch butterflies are great travelers.

Each fall they leave their homes in the

northern United States and Canada. *They head south for parts* of California, Florida, and Mexico. They make

one of Earth's greatest journeys.

A detail is added.

A sentence is moved to improve organization.

Think Like a Writer ★ Why would it be a good idea to take a break before you revise your first draft?

Focus

As you revise your work, pay attention to your subject, audience, and purpose. Take out or change anything that wanders from your topic. This is the time to move ideas, add details, and change words.

Language

While you are revising what you have written, take time to improve the language of your writing. Start with the beginning of your work. Make sure it catches your reader's interest.

Use verbs, adjectives, and adverbs that appeal to your reader's senses. Make your reader see, hear, smell, taste, and feel what you are describing.

Revising Marks

≡   capitalize
∧   add
  remove
⊙   add a period
/   make lowercase
  move
  transpose

Are you a good traveler? Believe it or not, you're not nearly as good as a monarch butterfly.

∧Monarch butterflies are great travelers.

The opening sentence is changed to grab the reader's attention.

Swarms   black and yellow   cling

∧Groups of butterflies attach themselves to branches.

Vivid words are added to improve language.

Think Like a Writer

★ Why should you think about your purpose and audience before you decide to add more details about your subject?

★ How can using good describing words make your writing better? Mark any changes you want to make on your first draft. You can save time by using revising marks.

Conferencing

Read your draft to a partner. Often another person can hear and see things in your writing that you have missed. Pay close attention when your partner gives an idea. Decide if you agree or not. One idea can lead to another.

> Is there a better word I could have used?

> Did I stay on the subject?

> Do you get my main idea?

> Did I leave anything out?

> Do I really need all these facts?

Making Changes

Mark any changes you want to make on your draft. You can save time by using revising marks. After marking your changes, copy your writing on a new sheet of paper.

Think Like a Writer

★ Why is it important to listen to everything your partner says?

★ Why is it easy for writers to make corrections and changes in their first draft on a computer?

Polish Your Writing

Editing and proofreading is the stage of the writing process when you get your writing ready to share or publish.

Read your writing several times. Look for a different kind of mistake each time you read. You want your writing to read smoothly and be free of errors.

Think Like a Writer

★ Why does reading your writing aloud to yourself or to a partner help you?

Grammar and Usage

The first time you proofread your writing, check for grammar and usage. Make sure each sentence has a subject, a predicate, and expresses a complete thought.

> Not many adult butterflies live to make the
>
> whole trip back and forth many in fact die,
>
> but females lay eggs Along the way.

Missing punctuation and capitalization are added.

A sentence is corrected.

Make your writing as smooth as possible. Combine sentences when you have several short, choppy sentences in a row. A short sentence can be expanded by adding details.

Writer's Tip
A good source for grammar rules is the *Writer's Handbook* section, on pages 224–245 of this book.

> quickly
> New butterflies are born. They grow. Soon
>
> and   long
> they fly. They land finish their parents' journey.

Sentences are expanded by adding details.

Two short, choppy sentences are combined.

Proofreading Marks

- ¶ indent first line of paragraph
- ≡ capitalize
- ^ or V add
- remove
- ⊙ add a period
- / make lowercase
- spelling mistake
- move
- transpose

Mechanics

Check your writing a second time to correct errors in mechanics. Capitalization and punctuation are the part of writing that is called mechanics.

Capitalization

Look over your writing, checking for words that should be capitalized. A capital letter signals a word of importance, such as a person's name, a title, place names, dates, and holidays.

For help with capitalization, turn to pages 246–250 in the *Writer's Handbook* section of this book.

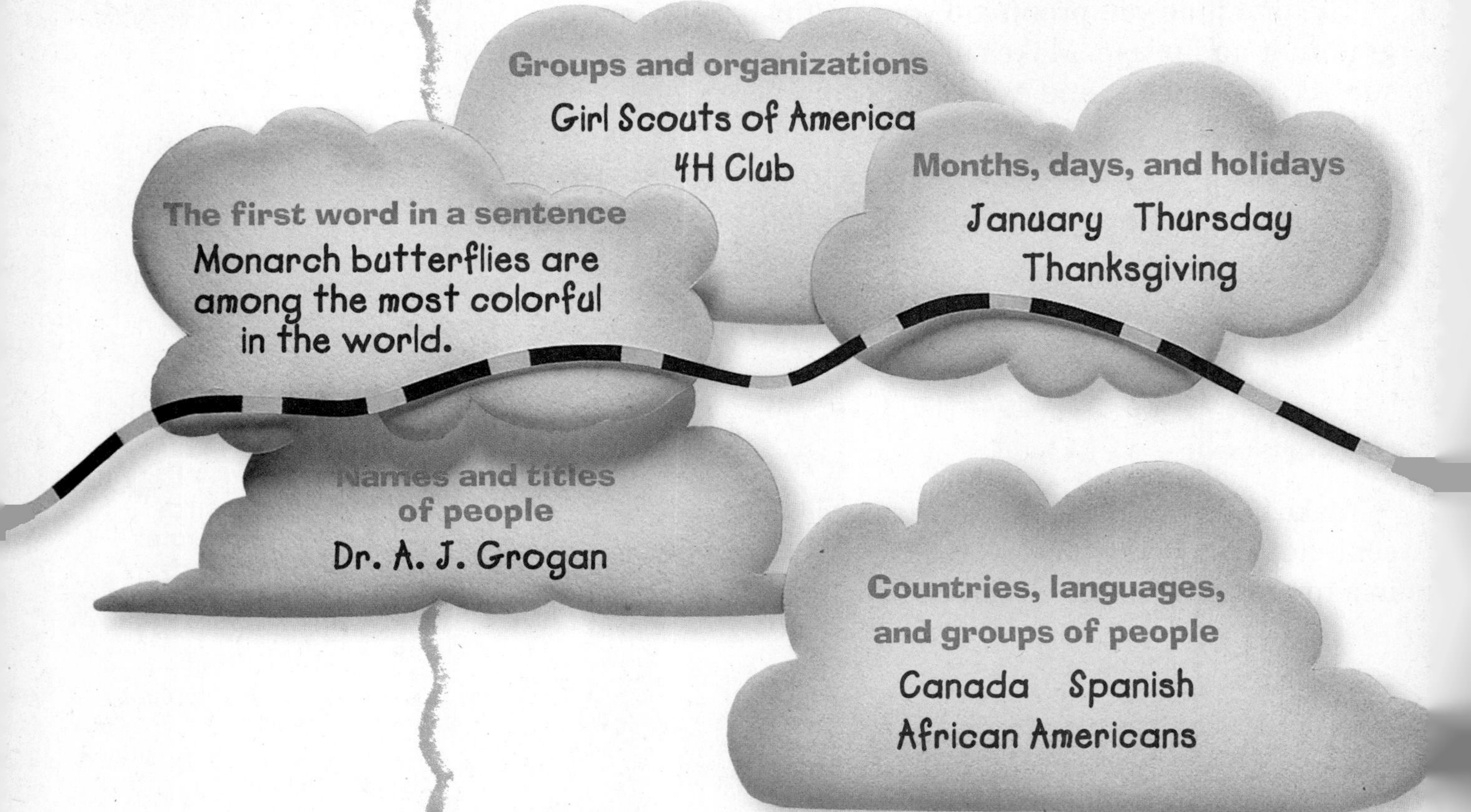
Groups and organizations
Girl Scouts of America
4H Club
Months, days, and holidays
January Thursday
Thanksgiving
The first word in a sentence
Monarch butterflies are among the most colorful in the world.
Names and titles of people
Dr. A. J. Grogan
Countries, languages, and groups of people
Canada Spanish
African Americans

Punctuation

Check your writing again for punctuation. Careful writers know when to use a period, a question mark, a comma, an apostrophe, quotation marks, and other forms of punctuation. You will find help with punctuation on pages 251–257 in the *Writer's Handbook* section.

Spelling

Finally, proofread your writing for spelling errors. Check words you are not sure how to spell. If you found the word when you gathered information, check the book or magazine in which you found it. You can also check spellings in a dictionary.

You will find more information about spelling rules and special tips in the *Writer's Handbook* section, on pages 259–268 of this book.

Checking for spelling errors will be easier if you keep a personal spelling dictionary. In it, place all the words you have just learned to spell.

M
Mexico
migrate
monarch

Spelling Dictionary

M
N
O
P
Q
R
S
T
U

Appearance

Can you imagine reading a book that had sloppy printing, scribble marks, and eraser marks all over it? Neatness counts!

Once you finish editing and proofreading your work, make a final copy. Work slowly so that you don't leave anything out. If you are writing by hand, use your best penmanship. If you are using a computer, make sure your copy looks right on the page.

Share Your Work

The final stage of the process of writing is publishing. After all the planning, revising, editing, and proofreading, writers are eager to let their readers be entertained or informed by their words and ideas.

How do you usually share a piece of writing with classmates or family members? Publishing can take many forms.

Printed Forms

Magazines and Newspapers

You and your classmates can share your writing by creating a class magazine, newspaper, or newsletter to publish all your stories or articles. Make copies for the whole school to read.

Butterfly Buz-z

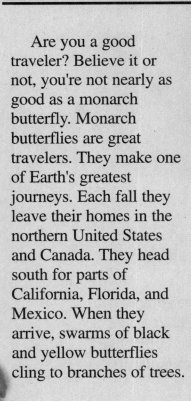

Are you a good traveler? Believe it or not, you're not nearly as good as a monarch butterfly. Monarch butterflies are great travelers. They make one of Earth's greatest journeys. Each fall they leave their homes in the northern United States and Canada. They head south for parts of California, Florida, and Mexico. When they arrive, swarms of black and yellow butterflies cling to branches of trees.

Not many adult butterflies live to make the whole trip back and forth. Many in fact die, but females lay eggs along the way. New butterflies are born. They grow quickly. Soon they fly and finish their parents' long journey. When spring comes, the monarchs return home once again.

Books

There are all sorts of books you can create to publish your writing. Plan how much writing will go on each page, add drawings or photographs, and create a cover.

Decide how you will fasten the pages together. You might choose a book with pages that flip from right to left, or pages that flip up or fold out like an accordion. Your entire book might be in the shape of your topic.

Experiment With Other Forms

When you publish, you are only limited by your imagination.

Here are some other ideas for sharing your work.

- **Bulletin Board** Create a display with your writing. Add illustrations, photos, graphs, or charts to get your point across.

- **Mail It** Make your own stationery, create a greeting card or postcard, and mail your writing to a friend.

- **Posters** Print your writing on a poster. Stand it on an easel or tape it to a wall.

Using Technology

Computers are a great tool for publishing. You can design a page to look a certain way and make several copies with the click of a mouse. You can even E-mail your writing to a friend in a flash.

Here are some technology tips.

- Add headlines, titles, and fancy covers.

- Make drawings or create charts and graphs.

Tech Tip
- Dress up your writing with different styles of type.
- Include pictures from the Internet or scan in a photo.

Migrating Monarchs
by Abby Ikeda

Are you a good traveler? Believe it or not, you're not nearly as good as a monarch butterfly. Monarch butterflies are great travelers. They make one of Earth's greatest journeys. Each fall they leave their homes in the northern United States and Canada. They head south for parts of California, Florida, and Mexico. When they arrive, swarms of black and yellow butterflies cling to branches of trees.

Presentations and Performances

Not all writing needs to be published in a handwritten or printed form. You can publish your work as an oral report, a speech, or a performance.

Oral Reports

In an oral report, you tell others about a subject you have written about. A report usually tries to inform people about something they do not know about yet.

Speeches

When you give a speech, you share an idea or opinion. Usually, a speech tries to persuade, or convince, people to think or act in a certain way.

Tips for Oral Reports and Speeches

- Use charts or graphs to show information.
- Use drawings or photos to get your point across.
- Look at your audience as you speak.
- Don't read your words. Talk to your audience.
- Use notes to keep you on the right track.

Performances

You might enjoy performing the story, tall tale, poem, or play scene you have written. Create scenery, wear costumes, hold props, or make puppets to share your writing. You can also make a tape recording or a videotape for your audience to listen to or view.

Think Like a Writer

★ What makes one kind of writing work best as a book and another as a poster, a play, or a speech?

★ How will you decide which pieces of writing should be published?

THE FORMS OF WRITING

TAKE NOTE

Writing to Learn

Writing Notes and Lists

Only people with photographic memories can remember everything they read. Most people need to write things down. A useful way to organize and record important information about a subject is to take notes or make a list.

Mavis takes **notes** on index cards. At the top of each note card, she writes the name of the book and page number to show where she got the information. She then writes important facts she wants to remember on the cards.

Meet the Writer

Using my note cards and making lists have improved my study skills.

Mavis Chen
California

Home Planet Earth, page 12
The equator is an imaginary line around the earth.
Equator runs from east to west.
Equator is halfway between the North Pole and the South Pole.

Note Card

Making a **list** is one way that Mavis brainstorms writing topics. Once she chooses a topic, she plans her writing by listing all the things she knows about the topic. She adds to the list until she can't think of any more ideas.

Maps show		Maps have
countries	oceans	a scale
states	roads	a compass rose
cities	rivers	

List

Talk About the Models

★ What does the writer include when taking notes?

★ How does the writer use a list to plan what she is going to write?

Your Turn

Make notes or a list to study for your next test. Write down all the important information you need to remember. Carry your notes with you. Pull them out to read whenever you have a chance.

Writing Log Entries

Meet the Writer

In my log, I write freely about subjects I am learning and experiences I have in school. Writing in a log gives me ideas for my own writing.

Kareem Dorsey
Michigan

Have you ever heard the expression "as easy as falling off a log"? Writing to learn is as easy as writing in a **log**. This log is a notebook where you can write down ideas, questions, or notes about subjects you are studying.

One way to organize your log is to use tabs to divide it into sections. You might label sections for literature, science, math, social studies, health, and language arts. One last section can be for observations.

Literature Log

When Kareem writes in his **literature log,** he records what he thinks and feels about books, stories, and poems he has read. He includes descriptions or quotations he wants to remember.

> May 23
>
> The Secret Moose by Jean Rogers
>
> Gerald secretly feeds a wounded moose in the woods near his home and helps the moose get better. I don't know if I could be brave enough to go into the woods with a wild animal.
>
> Literature Log

Literature · Science · Math · Social Studies · Health · Language Arts · Observations

Talk About the Model

★ What does the writer include in a log so he will remember the book he has read?

★ How will a literature log be helpful to the writer?

Learning Log

Kareem uses a large section of his notebook as a **learning log**. He has divided his learning log into sections that he labeled science, math, social studies, health, and language arts.

Kareem uses his learning log to keep track of what he knows and what he still needs to work on for each of his school subjects. He also writes questions he has about his subjects.

- He keeps track of new vocabulary words in his language arts log.

- He jots down key ideas from each chapter he reads for social studies and science.

- His math log is a great place for sample problems and drawing graphs.

- After a health lesson, he writes a summary or new vocabulary to learn.

Talk About the Model

★ How might the writer use the information he recorded for social studies?

★ How will writing questions help the writer become a better learner?

May 27

Natural Wonder
The Grand Canyon in Arizona
- 277 miles long
- 18 miles wide
- 1 mile deep
Old Faithful geyser in Wyoming
- shoots hot water and steam about every hour
- sprays 10,000 gallons of water at one time
Why does it erupt like that?

Learning Log

Literature · Science · Math · Social Studies · Health · Language Arts · Observations

Writer's Tip
Plan to spend more time writing about subjects that you find more difficult.

Observation Log

One last section of Kareem's notebook is used for recording **observations**. He draws and writes about what he notices about the world around him and the topics he studies in school. Whether he is eating lunch or doing a science experiment, he can record what is happening.

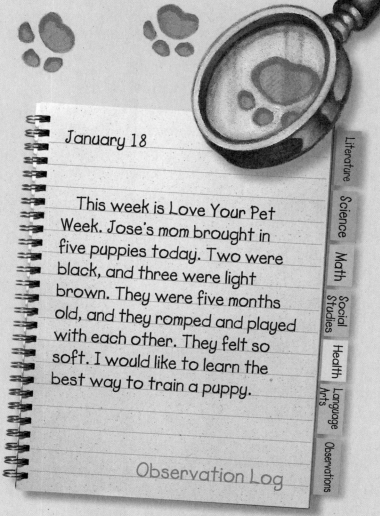

January 18

This week is Love Your Pet Week. Jose's mom brought in five puppies today. Two were black, and three were light brown. They were five months old, and they romped and played with each other. They felt so soft. I would like to learn the best way to train a puppy.

Observation Log

Tabs: Literature, Science, Math, Social Studies, Health, Language Arts, Observations

Talk About the Model

★ What experience does the writer record in his observation log?

★ Which details tell exactly what the writer observed?

Your Turn

Set up your own log.

Divide a notebook into sections, using paper or plastic tabs. Label the sections *Literature Log, Learning Log,* and *Observation Log.* You can also use a different notebook for each log if you want.

- Date each entry. Think and write freely. Include facts, feelings, and questions.
- Talk about what you write. Explain how new information fits with what you already know.

Writing Journal Entries

A **journal** is your special private notebook where you write about experiences, memories, feelings, and ideas. You can include notes, drawings, and doodles. You can write a lot or a little at a time—it all depends on what's important to you at the moment.

Meet the Writer

I write in my journal every day. I don't worry about what to say or how to say it.

Chris Nessler
Oklahoma

Debra   Me

June 28
I went to camp last week with my best friend. One night we stayed up too late talking. Suddenly the door opened, and there was the counselor. I really thought we were going to get into trouble. Ms. Nakai was very understanding and told us it was time to get some sleep.

Journal Entry

Each time Chris writes an entry in her journal, she begins with the date. In this way she can keep track of when things happened. She has found that her journal is a great place to look for writing ideas.

Talk About the Model

★ What reason did the writer have for writing this entry?

★ What does the writer do to keep track of when things happened to her?

Your Turn

- Use a special book for your journal.
- Write what comes to your mind.
- Include notes or drawings about your memories.

Writing Paragraphs

A **paragraph** is a group of sentences that tells about a main idea. The subject is often stated in the topic sentence. Sometimes this is the first sentence. The middle of a paragraph has detail sentences that give readers a clear picture of the topic. A closing sentence sums up the information.

The four kinds of paragraphs are narrative, descriptive, expository, and persuasive. Each kind of paragraph has its own purpose.

Narrative Paragraph

Mateo writes a **narrative paragraph** to tell a real or imagined story. Events are told in order of time.

> I've never been a great fan of plays, until last night. I went to a play with my friend and his family. We had great seats near the stage. During the first act, my friend and I were brought up on stage along with ten other kids. Before we knew it, we were wearing silly hats and masks and became characters in the play. A play is great fun when the audience participates. I can't wait until the next show!

Descriptive Paragraph

Mateo writes a **descriptive paragraph** to tell what a person, place, thing, or event is like. He includes details to help readers see, hear, smell, and feel his experience.

> I felt excited the second I heard the crack of the bat. Everything disappeared but the ball. I stopped smelling popcorn or hearing the crowd. I just saw the ball get bigger. I reached up to grab it. Thwap! It went right into my hands. My friends slapped me on the back and said, "Good job!" I felt so proud that day.

Meet the Writer

I always ask myself *who, what, when, where, why,* and *how.* This way I don't leave out any important details when I write a paragraph.

Mateo Hernandez
New York

Expository Paragraph

When Mateo's purpose is to give information about a subject, he writes an **expository paragraph**. He might explain an idea, present facts about a subject, or give directions.

Writer's Tip
Make your topic sentence fit the kind of paragraph you write.

> In the 1960s a high jumper named Dick Fosbury invented a new technique for high jumping. He called it the Fosbury Flop. As he jumped into the air, he twisted his body and went over the bar backward and head first. It was a weird way to jump, but Dick Fosbury won an Olympic gold medal.

Persuasive Paragraph

If he wants to convince readers to agree with his ideas and opinions, Mateo writes a **persuasive paragraph**. The facts and examples he includes will help prove that he is right.

> Travel is fun and educational. You meet interesting people and visit interesting places. Always stop by the visitor's center. The people who work there can give you tips about the best sights to see. In my opinion, a firsthand experience in a new place is the best way to learn.

Talk About the Models

★ How does the writer make you feel as if you were there at the play and the ball game?

★ What purpose does the writer have for writing about Dick Fosbury?

★ What does the writer say to convince you that travel is fun and educational?

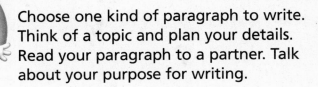

Choose one kind of paragraph to write. Think of a topic and plan your details. Read your paragraph to a partner. Talk about your purpose for writing.

Writing Summaries

You do a lot of reading every day including chapters, stories, articles, and printed material from your teacher. One way to remember all the important information you read is to write a **summary.**

When you write a summary, you choose the important ideas of a topic and write them in one clear paragraph. Your summary shows how clearly you understand what you've read.

Jeffrey wanted to learn about comets. First he found a reference book and read this article about comets. He did not want to write down everything he read, so he chose only the most important details. Then he wrote a summary using his own words.

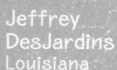

Meet the Writer

Writing a summary helps me decide what's important and what is not.

Jeffrey DesJardins
Louisiana

Comets

Comets are clouds of frozen gases, dust, rock, and ice. The largest comets are only a few miles across, but their tails can be millions of miles long.

The tail of a comet is made of glowing gases and dust particles. The tail looks very thick, but it is really quite fine. As a comet travels toward the sun, particles are knocked out of the comet and pushed away to form a long tail. Comets travel around the solar system in paths called orbits. At times they are very close to the sun, and at other times they are out beyond the farthest planet, Pluto. The complete orbit of a comet is called its period. The periods of different comets can vary quite a bit. One comet's period might be three and a half years, while another's might be 76 years. The periods of other comets might be centuries long.

Reference Article

Comets

Comets are clouds of frozen gases, dust, rock, and ice. They are a few miles across but have long tails made of gas and dust. Comets travel around the sun in an orbit. The time it takes for a comet to finish its orbit is called a period. A period can take a few years or many years.

Summary

Talk About the Model

★ How does the writer decide what to include in the summary?

★ Does the summary give enough information to give a clear picture of what a comet is? Why or why not?

Pick a nonfiction book and find an interesting chapter to read. Write a summary of what you read.

- Find the most important or main idea in each paragraph you read.
- Begin your summary with a sentence that states the main idea in your own words.
- Write down only important information.
- Arrange the details in an order that makes sense.
- Share your summary. See if your partner understands the main ideas of the selection you have read.

Writer's Tip
Compare your summary with the original to be sure you have included every important idea.

Writing Organizers, Charts, and Graphs

Meet the Writer

Before I write, I always use a diagram of some kind to collect and organize my thoughts.

Tina Chiago
Arizona

Have you ever used a sketch to help explain something to someone? Diagrams can help you organize your thoughts. Charts and graphs can present information in a clearer way than words alone.

Organizers

Tina uses a Venn diagram to show how two subjects are alike and different.

Tigers
live in Asia
striped coat

large cats
good hunters
sharp claws
for climbing,
catching
food, and for
protection

Lions
live mostly in
Africa
males have
manes

Venn Diagram

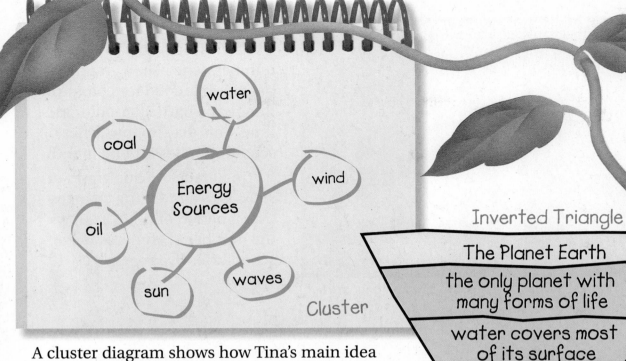

water

coal

Energy Sources

wind

oil

sun

waves

Cluster

Inverted Triangle

The Planet Earth

the only planet with many forms of life

water covers most of its surface

third planet from the sun

A cluster diagram shows how Tina's main idea and several details are connected.

An inverted, or upside-down, triangle helps her organize information from most important to least important.

Charts

Charts help Tina organize information and show how the details fit together. Every chart has rows (going across) and columns (going up and down). Tina made this chart to organize information about rain-forest animals.

Jungle Layers	Rain-Forest Animals
Emergent	great hornbill birdwing butterfly
Canopy	black spider monkey sloth
Understory	aye-aye emerald tree boa
Floor	giant armadillo giant anteater
River	capybara caiman

Chart

Writer's Tip
The kind of diagram you use depends on how you want to organize your topic.

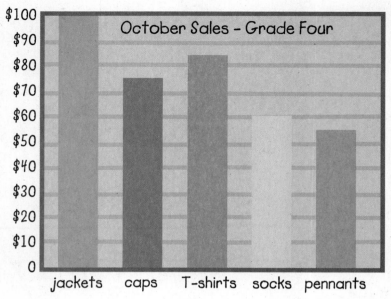

October Sales - Grade Four

$100
$90
$80
$70
$60
$50
$40
$30
$20
$10
0

jackets   caps   T-shirts   socks   pennants

Bar Graph

Graphs

When Tina wants to explain numbers, she uses a graph. A bar graph is good for comparing things at a particular point in time. This graph shows sales of school supplies for one month.

Tina made the line graph to show how something changes over a period of time. It shows the number of students in her school over five years.

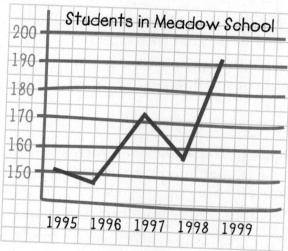

Students in Meadow School

200
190
180
170
160
150

1995   1996   1997   1998   1999

Line Graph

Talk About the Models

★ How can the writer use an organizer to plan for writing?

★ What does the writer do to make the information on the chart easy to read and understand?

★ Why are graphs and charts a helpful way to publish information?

Your Turn

Work in a small group. Choose an interesting topic that involves numbers.

• Collect your information.

• Present it in an organizer, a chart, or a graph.

ONCE UPON A TIME

Writing to Tell a Story

Writing a Narrative Paragraph

In a **narrative paragraph**, the writer tells a story about something that actually happened. The characters, setting, and events are all real. In "Ice Skating," Toby tells about the first time she and her friends went skating last winter. Her teacher said her choice of words and the details she included brought her story to life.

Meet the Writer

I can't wait for winter so my friends and I can go ice skating. I wrote this paragraph about the day when the ice on the pond was finally ready for skating.

Toby Barna
New Jersey

Hi, I'm Toby.

Ice Skating
by Toby Barna

I love to ice skate! In the winter I check the park every day to see if the pond is frozen yet. Finally, one day in December, I looked and looked, but I couldn't find the big serious sign that screamed, "NO SKATING!" I was very excited. I ran home and called my two best friends, Angela and Brooke, to see if they wanted to go skating. We all sat on a bench and put on our skates. We were all so excited that we just ran out and leapt onto the ice. We glided two feet and PLOP! We fell on the ice in a heap. What a beginning!

Talk About the Model

★ How does the writer let you know what the paragraph is about?

★ Which sentences give interesting details?

★ Which sentences tell you how Toby feels about skating?

Make a Plan

Now it's your turn to write. Start by making a plan.

- Who or what will you write about? Keep your subject simple so that you can tell about it in one paragraph.
- Who is your audience? Remember that your audience may not know anything about your subject.
- What details will you include? The details in your supporting sentences tell your story and keep your reader interested.

Write It Down

- Begin your paragraph by writing a topic sentence. Remember to indent.
- Tell what happened in order. Words like *first*, *next*, and *last* may help you.
- Stick to your topic.

Conferencing

Read your narrative paragraph to a partner. Is there anything else your partner needs to know?

Look It Over

Read your paragraph. Is your writing interesting and clear? Did you include enough details about your experience? Did you check your spelling?

Tech Tip

If you are using a computer, use the Cut and Paste tools to move a sentence or a word.

Portfolio

File your paragraph. You might decide to revise, edit, proofread, and publish your paragraph.

Writing a Realistic Story

Put together characters who seem real, a setting that could really exist, and events that could happen, and you have the ingredients for a realistic story. The ideas for such a story often come from the writer's own experiences and interests.

The book *Every Living Thing* by Cynthia Rylant is an example of realistic fiction. In this passage the writer introduces her readers to the members of the Lacey family and the puppy that wanders into their life.

The writer captures the reader's interest.

The setting and characters could really exist.

In January, a puppy wandered onto the property of Mr. Amos Lacey and his wife, Mamie, and their daughter, Doris. The puppy had been abandoned, and it made its way down the road toward the Lacey's small house, its ears tucked, its tail between its legs, shivering.

Meet the Writer

Cynthia Rylant has written dozens of books for young people. Her series of books about Henry and Mudge is the most popular.

EVERY LIVING THING
STORIES BY
Cynthia Rylant
DECORATIONS BY
S.D. Schindler

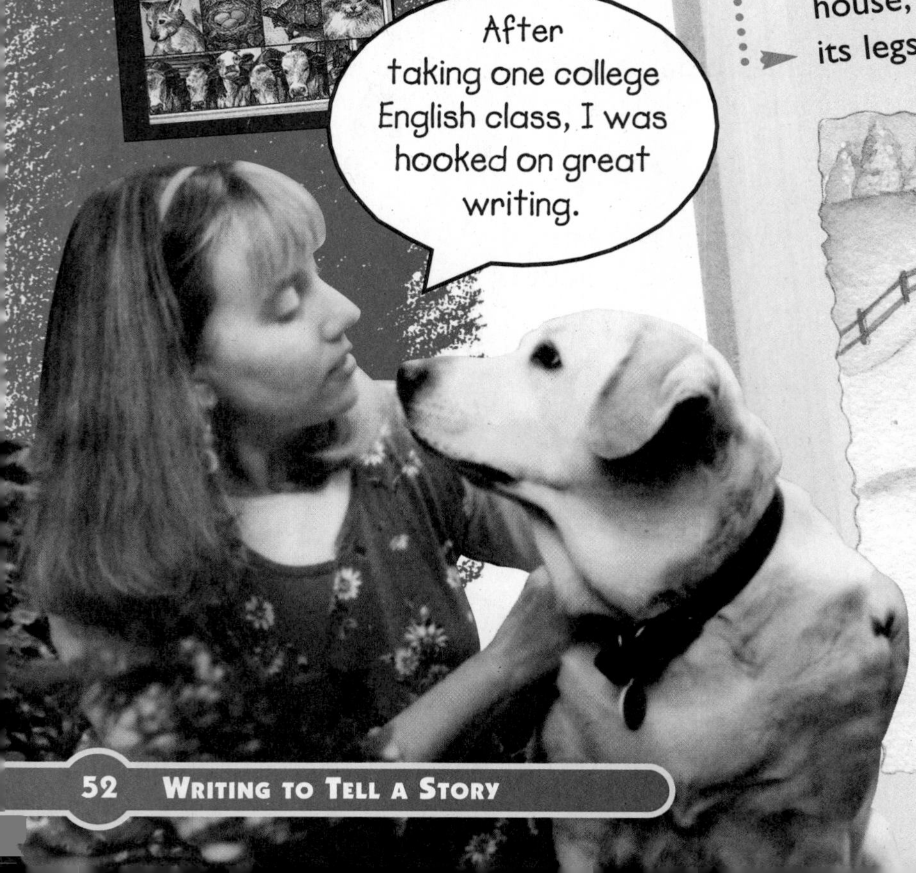

After taking one college English class, I was hooked on great writing.

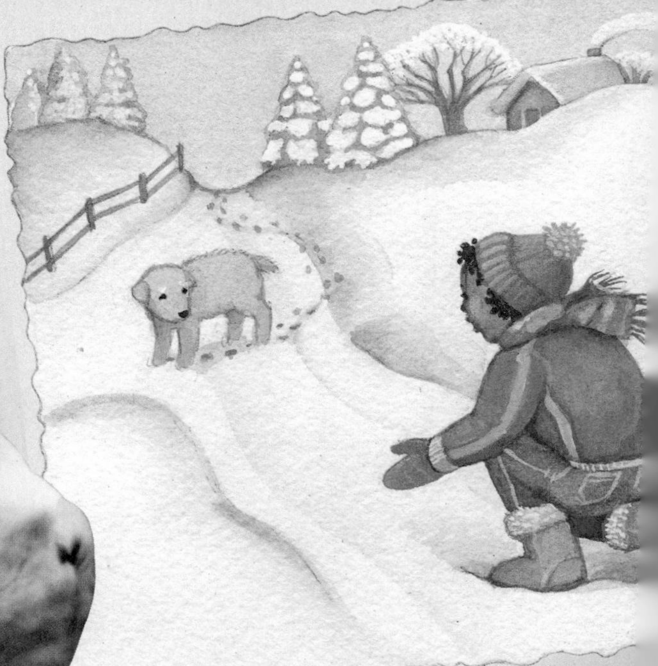

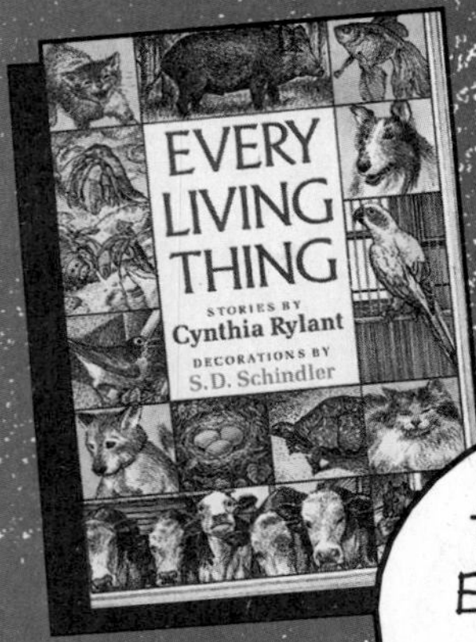

Talk About the Model

As a Reader

★ What captures your attention in this passage?

★ Would you be interested in reading the rest of this story? Why or why not?

As a Writer

★ What details does the writer include to make the setting seem real?

★ What makes the characters and actions believable?

★ How do you think the writer got the idea for this story?

Doris, whose school had been called off because of the snow, was out shoveling the cinderblock front steps when she spotted the pup on the road. She set down the shovel.

"Hey! Come on!" she called.

The puppy stopped in the road, wagging its tail timidly, trembling with shyness and cold. Doris trudged through the yard, went up the shoveled drive and met the dog.

"Come on, Pooch."

"Where did that come from?" Mrs. Lacey asked as soon as Doris put the dog down in the kitchen.

Mr. Lacey was at the table, cleaning his fingernails with his pocketknife. The snow was keeping him home from his job at the warehouse.

"I don't know where it came from," he said mildly, "but I know for sure where it's going."

Doris hugged the puppy hard against her. She said nothing.

> The writer uses dialogue to make the situation come alive.

> Details help the readers know the main character.

> A believable problem is introduced.

Make a Plan

Before you write a realistic story, do a quick write to jot down your ideas.

- Give your character a name and tell about his or her looks, personality, likes, and dislikes.
- Describe your setting. Picture your character in a place just like your school or neighborhood.
- Come up with a problem for your character to solve. It can be exciting, serious, or funny.
- Organize your story. Decide which events will happen first, next, and last.

Write It Down

Begin with something that will catch your readers' interest. It might be a statement about the character and situation or a conversation between characters.

Tell what happens in a logical order. Include lots of dialogue to keep your readers interested. End the story by telling how the problem is solved.

Tech Tip

If you are using a computer, print extra copies to share with your family and friends.

Conferencing

Read your story to a small group. Ask if your story is entertaining and interesting.

Look It Over

Reread your story. Are you happy with it? You always can go back to add or make changes.

Portfolio

Keep your story and notes or drawings. They'll be useful if you decide to publish.

A Story Starring Me!

Some writers create stories about themselves. The characters, places, and events are all from real-life experiences. When you write a true story about yourself, it is called a **personal narrative.**

A Personal Narrative

★ **Has one topic that tells about the writer**

★ **Describes a problem the writer has and how the problem is solved**

★ **Uses words such as *I*, *me*, and *my* to tell about the writer**

★ **Tells events in the order in which they happened**

★ **Is a story with a beginning, a middle, and an end**

★ **Includes dialogue to make characters seem real**

Meet the Writer

I love the ocean. Two years ago I went on a glass-bottom boat with my family. I had such a good time I wanted to share it with my friends. So I wrote a story about my ride.

Michael Dalsass
New Jersey

Think It Through

The first step in writing a personal narrative is to choose a topic. Check out your journal or log for ideas. Next, gather information about the topic. Then, think through what you want to say about it.

Brainstorming

What do you remember about an event in your life? One way to find out is to use your feelings as a guide.

Your Turn

> List the following adjectives on a sheet of paper.
>
> happy   excited   embarrassed
> scared   sad   proud
> nervous   angry   lonely
>
> Next to each word, write about an experience or event when you felt this way.

Michael's List

Happy—going to a baseball game for my birthday

Excited—my first trip on a glass-bottom boat

Embarrassed—the day my science demonstration didn't work

Select a Topic

Look at your list of memorable experiences.

- Which memories are your favorites?
- Which experiences do you remember in the most detail?
- Which memories do you enjoy sharing with others?

Choose the most interesting idea as a topic for your personal narrative.

Design a Plan

Michael made a story map to plan his personal narrative. Read his plan to find out what goes in the beginning, middle, and end of his story.

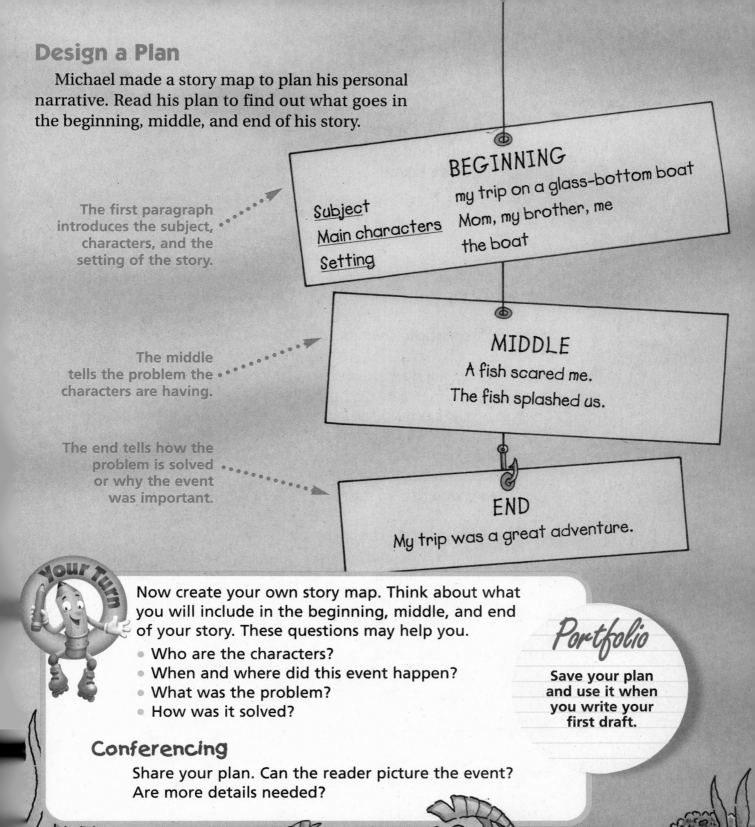

The first paragraph introduces the subject, characters, and the setting of the story.

BEGINNING
my trip on a glass-bottom boat
Subject
Main characters   Mom, my brother, me
Setting   the boat

The middle tells the problem the characters are having.

MIDDLE
A fish scared me.
The fish splashed us.

The end tells how the problem is solved or why the event was important.

END
My trip was a great adventure.

Your Turn

Now create your own story map. Think about what you will include in the beginning, middle, and end of your story. These questions may help you.

- Who are the characters?
- When and where did this event happen?
- What was the problem?
- How was it solved?

Conferencing

Share your plan. Can the reader picture the event? Are more details needed?

Portfolio

Save your plan and use it when you write your first draft.

PERSONAL NARRATIVE
Drafting

Put It Into Words

The narrative below is Michael's first draft. He wanted to write down as much information as he could remember. Does his trip remind you of one you've taken?

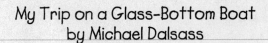

My Trip on a Glass-Bottom Boat
by Michael Dalsass

Beginning

Two years ago my mom, my brother, and I took a trip on a glass-bottom boat. The big boat was made of wood and was painted gray. My mom, my brother, and I could see through the bottom of the boat to the ocean floor. The sun was blazing and we had to wear sunglasses.

Middle

I saw a huge fish swimming below us that was over six feet long! I yelled, "Aaahh!" The guide said, "It's only a barracuda." A guide told us about all kinds of fish. Next I saw a school of fish named amberjack. The guide threw food into the crystle clear water, and the fish leapt into the air like monarch butterflies. As the fish fell back into the water, the fish splashed all the tourists.

End

We took a lot of photos that day. When I look at them, I think about my great adventur. If you want to see ocean creatures up close, a glass-bottom boat is the place to be!

Think Like a Writer

As you write your first draft, ask yourself these questions.

★ **Subject:** What event am I focusing on?

★ **Audience:** Who will read what I write?

★ **Purpose:** What is my goal?

★ **Form:** What are the characteristics of a personal narrative?

Now you're ready to write the first draft of your personal narrative. Stick to your plan. Don't worry about making mistakes or leaving out any details. You can go back and make changes later. Use the following list as a guide.

Drafting Checklist

- You are the main character. Write in the first person, using the pronoun "I."
- The first paragraph introduces the characters and describes the setting.
- The middle of the story describes the problem the characters had.
- The last paragraph ends the story by telling how everything worked out and what you learned from your experience.
- Brainstorm titles for your story. Choose the one you like best.

Conferencing

Read your first draft to a partner. Did you capture your partner's interest? How can you improve your personal narrative?

Revising
Take Another Look

After Michael wrote his first draft, he decided to make some changes. Look at the draft below. What changes were made? How do you think they improved Michael's personal narrative?

Start with a question to get the reader's attention. · · · ▶

Use a word that tells more about the boat. · · · · · · · · ▶

Take out unimportant information. · · · ▶

Put the topic sentence at the beginning of the paragraph. · · · · ▶

Add dialogue to make the characters seem real. · · · ▶

My Trip on a Glass-Bottom Boat
by Michael Dalsass

Would you like to look at ocean creatures without getting wet?
Two years ago my mom, my brother, and I took a trip on a

two-story
glass-bottom boat. The big boat was made of wood and was

painted gray. My mom, my brother, and I could see through the

bottom of the boat to the ocean floor. ~~The sun was blazing~~

~~and we had to wear sunglasses.~~

I saw a huge fish swimming below us that was over six feet

long! I yelled, "Aaahh!" The guide said, "It's only a barracuda." A

guide told us about all kinds of fish. Next I saw a school of fish

named amberjack. The guide threw food into the crystle clear

water, and the fish leapt into the air like monarch butterflies. As

the fish fell back into the water, the fish splashed all the tourists.

I laughed and said, "thanks! That cool water feels refreshing!"
We took a lot of photos that day. When I look at them, I think

about my great adventur. If you want to see ocean creatures

up close, a glass-bottom boat is the place to be!

Read your personal narrative to yourself. What do you like about your writing? What changes could you make to improve it?

Don't worry about marking up your draft. This is the time to make notes in the margin, cross out words, and add details. You may need to revise your writing more than once. Use the Revising Checklist to help you decide what changes to make.

Revising Checklist

- Is the story told from the writer's point of view?
- Does the story tell about a problem the characters had and how they solved it?
- Are there details about the characters and the setting?
- Is dialogue used to make the story more interesting?
- Does the story tell how the writer and others felt?

Conferencing

Ask a partner to read your personal narrative and to answer the Revising Checklist questions. If your partner answers *no* to any questions, talk about what was unclear or missing and possible changes you could make.

Become a Super Writer

To make your writing more interesting, use dialogue. For help, see the *Writer's Handbook* section, page 209.

Revising Marks

≡ capitalize
∧ add
◞ remove
⊙ add a period
／ make lowercase
○ move
∼ transpose

Tech Tip
Use the Cut and Paste tools of your program to move words. Ask your teacher how to save each revision.

Portfolio

Save your revisions in your portfolio until you are ready to edit and proofread your writing.

Polish Your Writing

After several revisions, Michael was happy with his story. With a few small corrections, he will be all finished! Proofreading marks make correcting easier.

My Trip on a Glass-Bottom Boat
by Michael Dalsass

Would you like to look at ocean creatures without getting

wet? Two years ago my mom, my brother, and I took a trip on a

glass-bottom boat. The two-story boat was made of wood and

We

was painted gray. ~~My mom, my brother, and~~ I could see through the

it

bottom of the ~~boat~~ to the ocean floor.

Replace nouns with a subject pronoun.

Replace a noun with an object pronoun.

A guide told us about all kinds of fish. I saw a huge fish

swimming below us that was over six feet long! I yelled, "Aaahh!"

The guide said, "It's only a barracuda." Next I saw a school of

crystal

fish named amberjack. The guide threw food into the (crystle)

Correct a spelling mistake.

clear water, and the fish leapt into the air like monarch

they

butterflies. As the fish fell back into the water, ~~the fish~~

Replace a noun with a subject pronoun.

splashed all the tourists. I laughed and said, "thanks! That cool

water feels refreshing!"

Capitalize the first letter in a quotation.

We took a lot of photos that day. When I look at them, I think

adventure.

about my great (adventur) If you want to see ocean creatures

Correct another spelling mistake.

up close, a glass-bottom boat is the place to be!

Now it's your turn to edit and proofread your writing so that it will be ready to be published. Use a colored pencil and the proofreading marks to the right to show the changes you want to make. The Editing and Proofreading Checklist will help you.

Proofreading Marks

¶	indent first line of paragraph
≡	capitalize
∧ or ∨	add
ℛ	remove
⊙	add a period
/	make lowercase
◯	spelling mistake
↜	move
∼	transpose

Editing and Proofreading Checklist

- Did I use personal pronouns, such as "I," "me," and "my," correctly in sentences?
  See page 243 in the *Writer's Handbook* section.
- Did I use subject and object pronouns correctly?
  See page 242 in the *Writer's Handbook* section.
- Did I use capital letters at the beginning of quotations and sentences?
  See page 248 in the *Writer's Handbook* section.
- Did I spell all words correctly?
  See page 259 in the *Writer's Handbook* section.

Tech Tip
Use your computer's Spelling tool to double check your spelling. Remember to save your copy.

Conferencing

Ask a partner to edit and proofread again with you. Listen to suggestions your partner makes.

Portfolio
Keep your final draft in your folder until you are ready to publish it.

Become a Super Writer

Subject and object pronouns add variety in writing. For help, see the *Writer's Handbook* section, page 242.

Share Your Work

Michael's story is finished! After he made the corrections, he made a final copy. He decided to publish his story by making a story silhouette. This is how it looked.

My Trip on a Glass-Bottom Boat
by Michael Dalsass

Would you like to look at ocean creatures without getting wet? Two years ago my mom, my brother, and I took a trip on a glass-bottom boat. The two-story boat was made of wood and was painted gray. We could see through the bottom of it to the ocean floor.

A guide told us about all kinds of fish. I saw a huge fish swimming below us that was over six feet long! I yelled, "Aaahh!" The guide said, "It's only a barracuda." Next I saw a school of fish named amberjack. The guide threw food into the crystal clear water, and the fish leapt into the air like monarch butterflies. As the fish fell back into the water, they splashed all the tourists. I laughed and said, "Thanks! That cool water feels refreshing!"

We took a lot of photos that day. When I look at them, I think about my great adventure. If you want to see ocean creatures up close, a glass-bottom boat is the place to be!

Here are three very different ways to share your writing with your friends, family, and teachers.

Create a Story Silhouette ▶

Work with a partner to make a silhouette of your head.

- Tape a piece of paper to the wall and sit sideways in front of it.
- Shine a bright light so that it casts a shadow of your head on the paper.
- Have your partner trace the outline of your head on the paper.
- Cut out the silhouette and write your story on it.
- Glue it to a piece of dark paper.

◀ Tell It in Pictures

Create a picture album to tell your story.

- Glue photographs or drawings onto sheets of construction paper.
- Write a caption for each picture.
- Compile the pages to make an album.
- Create a cover.
- Share your story and picture album with the class.

Make a Speech ▶

Pretend you are a famous writer and you've been asked to give a speech about an interesting experience in your life. Use your personal narrative. You can read it word for word, or you can make notes and speak from them.

Creating a Comic Strip

Meet the Writer

Since 1950, Charles Schulz's *Peanuts* has been one of the world's most popular comic strips.

A **comic strip** is a series of drawings in frames that use words and pictures to tell a story. Some comic strips tell about "far-out" heroes and adventures, and others entertain readers with characters who say and do funny things. People who create comic strips are called cartoonists.

The comic strips on pages 66 and 67 are from *Peanuts* by Charles Schulz. Both appeared in newspapers just before Valentine's Day.

Two characters tell the story.

The characters say funny things.

PEANUTS reprinted by permission of United Feature Syndicate In

To take a blank piece of paper and draw characters that people love and worry about is extremely satisfying.

Talk About the Model

As a Reader

★ How does the cartoonist get you interested in the characters and what they are saying?

★ If it wasn't Valentine's Day, would you want to read these comic strips? Why or why not?

As a Writer

★ What special features does the cartoonist use to tell you what happens first, next, and last?

★ Does the cartoonist write about everyday life or a make-believe situation?

Each frame shows one part of the story line.

The dialogue is short and simple.

The cartoonist ends with a surprise.

PEANUTS

WHAT ARE YOU WRITING, MARCIE?

I'M SENDING A VALENTINE TO CHARLES.

YOU CAN'T DO THAT. HE'LL THINK YOU LIKE HIM.

I DO. I'M VERY FOND OF CHARLES.

WHY DON'T YOU SIGN MY NAME, TOO?

OH, SURE! HITCH A RIDE ON MY VALENTINE!

© 1998 United Feature Syndicate, Inc.

2-13

Make a Plan

It's your turn to be a cartoonist! Follow these steps to create your comic strip.

Choose What the Characters Do and Say

Jot down notes to plan which characters will appear in each frame of your comic strip, what they will say, and what happens.

Write It Down

- Draw three frames on paper.
- Draw your characters and setting in each frame.
- Add dialogue in speech balloons to tell the story.
- Show humor in what the characters say and do.
- End your story with a surprise.

Conferencing

Read your comic strip with a partner. Ask if the drawings and words clearly tell the story.

Tech Tip

If you are writing with a computer, use the Table tool to create your frames.

Look It Over

Read your comic strip again. Do the frames show a sequence? Does the dialogue fit each character's actions? Is there anything you could add to make your comic strip funnier? Check your sentences for capitalization and punctuation.

A Story That's BIGGER Than Life

Have you ever stretched the truth a bit when you told a story? Maybe you exaggerated what happened or made yourself seem bigger or stronger than you really are.

A fantasy story that uses exaggeration and humor to entertain the reader is called a **tall tale**. The pioneers often amused each other with tales of amazing adventures, featuring larger-than-life heroes such as Paul Bunyan, John Henry, Pecos Bill, and Slue-Foot Sue.

Meet the Writer

I like to imagine lots of things that could happen. My imagination keeps me from getting bored. I wrote this tall tale about my own superhero to entertain my classmates.

Lindsey McNeil
Texas

A Tall Tale

★ Is a fantasy story that is fun and entertaining
★ Tells about imaginary heroes and their adventures
★ Uses exaggeration and humor to describe the characters and what they do
★ Features a main character who usually has a problem to solve or a villain to defeat
★ Has a beginning, a middle, and an end

Think It Through

Begin to plan your tall tale by choosing a topic for your story. Once you decide who your tall-tale hero is, where your story takes place, and what the problem is, you are on your way to creating your tale.

Brainstorming

Think of an amazing hero your audience will enjoy reading about. What makes your hero larger than life? Is it his or her size or strength? Is your hero brave and smart?

Think about the problem your hero will face. Will it be a villain to defeat or a powerful force?

Imagine who your hero will be. Do a quick write to tell what your hero is like. Then write a list of problems your hero might help you face.

Lindsey's List

Character	Problems to Solve
Guy, my superhero dog	helps me when I get hurt
really clever	rescues me when I am bored
has wings to fly	protects me from dangers
is fun to be with	

Select a Topic

Look over the ideas you have written about your character and a story problem.

- What problem sounds the most exciting for a tall tale?
- What characteristics does your hero have to help you solve your problem?

Choose the most interesting idea as the topic for your tall tale.

Design a Plan

To help plan her tall tale, Lindsey made this chart for her story ideas. She included her characters, the setting, the problem, and the events of the story. This is what her plan looked like.

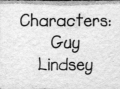

Characters:
Guy
Lindsey

Setting:
school
beach

Problem:
Lindsey was bored and tired in class the day before a math test.

Events:
1. Guy rescued Lindsey from class.
2. Guy put someone in Lindsey's seat at school.
3. Guy took Lindsey to the beach.
4. Lindsey went home and studied for her test.

Create your own story map. Ask yourself these questions.

- Who are my characters?
- What is my setting?
- What is my story problem?
- What are my story events?

Conferencing

Share your story map with a partner. What does your partner think of your superhero? Does your adventure sound extraordinary?

Portfolio

Save your story plan so you can use it when you write your first draft.

Put It Into Words

When Linsey wrote her first draft, her imagination was working overtime to get everything down on paper. What details did Lindsey include that let you know her story is a tall tale?

Super Dog Saves the Day
by Lindsey McNeil

If you are having a boring day, how about flying away with

The superhero is introduced. ▸ Guy, the superhero dog? Guy is five feet tall, with a round

furry body. He has wings, but nobody but his friend can see

them. He hears with his large ears whenever his friend Lindsey

Exaggeration describes what the hero is able to do. ▸ blows her secret whistel.

Guy rescue Lindsey whenever she needs help. He eats

vegetables she doesn't like. Once he rescued her on Math

The problem is identified. ▸ Review Day. Lindsey was bored and tired. She blew her whistel.

Guy appeared. He said he would put someone who looks just like

Lindsey in her seat and take her to the beach. At the beach,

The adventure sounds larger than life. ▸ Lindsey and Guy played in the waves and collected seashells.

Soon Lindsey's dad was going to pick her up at school. Guy

The adventure is told in a logical order. ▸ unfurled his wings and flew her back. At school, Guy lay down

outside and waited for Lindsey. Guy, Dad and Lindsey walked

home together. Lindsey studied hard for her math test.

The problem is solved. ▸ The next day she got an A⁺.

Think Like a Writer

Ask yourself these questions as you write your first draft.

★ **Subject:** What character is the focus of my tall tale?

★ **Audience:** Who will enjoy reading my entertaining tale?

★ **Purpose:** Why am I writing this tale?

★ **Form:** What are the characteristics of a tall tale?

Writer's Tip
If you are writing by hand, don't erase. Just cross out the words you don't want.

Your Turn

As you begin to write your first draft, follow your story idea chart. The most important thing is to get your ideas on paper. You can always go back over your draft later to make changes or add details. Here is a checklist to use as a guide.

Tech Tip
It's easy to cut or insert words until you have just the right words to describe your character.

Drafting Checklist

- Introduce your hero. Also introduce the villain, if you have one.
- Start off with action or dialogue that will make your audience eager to keep reading.
- Describe your hero's adventure in the middle of the tale. Include lots of humor and exaggeration.
- End your tall tale by telling how the hero saved the day.
- Give your tale an exciting title.

Portfolio
Take a break from your exciting hero. You can revise your tale later.

Conferencing

Read your first draft to a partner. Is your character "tall" enough and your problem "big" enough? Are the story details clear from beginning to end?

Take Another Look

Lindsey used the Drafting Checklist to make some changes. Her writing partner also gave her some ideas. How do you think Lindsey's changes improve her tale?

New opening sentence gets the reader's attention.

Descriptive words show exaggeration.

Delete a sentence that is off the topic.

Add information to show where the story takes place.

Add dialogue to make the tale more interesting.

Super Dog Saves the Day
by Lindsey McNeil

It's Guy, the super dog, to the rescue!

If you are having a boring day, how about flying away with Guy, the superhero dog? Guy is five feet tall, with a round long, feathery furry body. He has wings, but nobody but his friend can see them. He hears with his ~~large~~ elephant-like ears whenever his friend Lindsey blows her secret whistel.

Guy rescue Lindsey whenever she needs help. ~~He eats vegetables she doesn't like.~~ Once he rescued her on Math Review Day. Lindsey was bored and tired in class. She blew her whistel. Guy appeared ~~He said he would put someone who looks just like Lindsey in her seat and take her to the beach.~~ and said, "i'll take you away and put someone in your seat who looks just like you. Let's go to the beach!" At the beach, Lindsey and Guy played in the waves and collected seashells.

Soon Lindsey's dad was going to pick her up at school. Guy unfurled his wings and flew her back. At school, Guy lay down outside and waited for Lindsey. Guy, Dad and Lindsey walked home together. Lindsey studied hard for her math test.

The next day she got an A⁺.

Read over your own tall tale. Can you think of words and ideas to add? Are there any parts you want to take out? What other changes would you like to make? Use the Revising Checklist as a guide.

Revising Marks

≡	capitalize
∧	add
๑	remove
⊙	add a period
/	make lowercase
◡	move
∾	transpose

Revising Checklist

- Have I introduced and described my hero?
- Does the hero help solve a problem or defeat a villain?
- Have I used humor and exaggeration to tell my tale?
- Have I used dialogue to make the tale more interesting?
- Are events told in the correct sequence?
- Does my ending wrap up the events?

Tech Tip
Remember to save your document. You don't want to lose your tall tale in cyberspace!

Conferencing

Ask your partner to read your tall tale and answer the questions in the Revising Checklist. If your partner answers any questions with *no*, talk about the question and the changes you could make in your tale.

Portfolio
Store your revised draft. Return to it on another day to edit and proofread.

Become a Super Writer

Use exaggeration and humor to make your writing more fun for your reader. For help, see the *Writer's Handbook* section in this book, on pages 209–210.

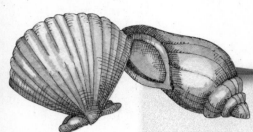

Polish Your Writing

After Lindsey revised her tall tale, she thought her story would entertain her readers. She read her draft again to make final corrections. What changes did Lindsey make?

Super Dog Saves the Day
by Lindsey McNeil

It's Guy, the super dog, to the rescue! If you are having a

boring day, how about flying away with Guy, the superhero

Add a comma. ···· dog? Guy is five feet tall, with a round furry body. He has

long, feathery wings, but nobody but his friend can see them.

Correct a spelling mistake. ···· He hears with his elephant-like ears whenever his friend Lindsey

whistle
blows her secret ~~whistel.~~

Make the subject and verb agree. ····
s
Guy rescue Lindsey whenever she needs help. Once he

rescued her on Math Review Day. Lindsey was bored and tired

whistle
in class. She blew her ~~whistel.~~ Guy appeared and said, "i'll take

Capitalize the first word in a quotation. ····
you away and put someone in your seat who looks just like you.

Let's go to the beach!" At the beach, Lindsey and Guy played in

the waves and collected seashells.

Soon Lindsey's dad was going to pick her up at school. Guy

Add a time-order word and replace nouns with a pronoun. ···· unfurled his wings and flew her back. At school, Guy lay down

Then they
outside and waited for Lindsey. ~~Guy, Dad and Lindsey~~ walked

home together. Lindsey studied hard for her math test.

The next day she got an A+.

Give your tall tale a final polish so that it is ready to be published. Remember, the proofreading marks will make it easier for you to mark changes. This Editing and Proofreading Checklist can be your guide.

Editing and Proofreading Checklist

- Do my subjects and verbs agree?
  See page 237 in the *Writer's Handbook* section.
- Did I use commas after introductory phrases?
  See page 255 in the *Writer's Handbook* section.
- Did I use capital letters with proper nouns?
  See page 246 in the *Writer's Handbook* section.
- Did I use quotation marks around dialogue?
  See page 257 in the *Writer's Handbook* section.

Conferencing

Share your edited tale with a partner.
Work together to proofread one more time.

Become a Super Writer

Correct sentence form means that subjects and verbs agree in number. For help with subject-verb agreement, see the *Writer's Handbook* section, page 237.

Proofreading Marks

升	indent first line of paragraph
≡	capitalize
∧ or ∨	add
⌀	remove
⊙	add a period
/	make lowercase
	spelling mistake
∽	move
∼	transpose

Tech Tip

Use your computer's Spelling and Grammar tools to give a final check to your tale.

Portfolio

Clip together your prewriting notes and drafts. They show the steps you took to reach your published tale.

Math A+

$$80.43$$
$$7.95$$
$$+ \ \ \ \ \ $$
$$\overline{88.38}$$

$$24.53$$
$$+ 25.81$$
$$\overline{50.34}$$

$$89.43$$
$$- 87.51$$
$$\overline{1.92}$$

$$74.63$$
$$- 66.96$$
$$\overline{7.67}$$

Share Your Work

Once Lindsey finished polishing her tall tale, she was ready to share it with others during a "campfire tale-a-thon." Read her final copy to see how well it turned out.

Super Dog Saves the Day
by Lindsey McNeil

It's Guy, the super dog, to the rescue! If you are having a boring day, how about flying away with Guy, the superhero dog? Guy is five feet tall, with a round, furry body. He has long, feathery wings, but nobody but his friend can see them. He hears with his elephant-like ears whenever his friend Lindsey blows her secret whistle.

Guy rescues Lindsey whenever she needs help. Once he rescued her on Math Review Day. Lindsey was bored and tired in class. She blew her whistle. Guy appeared and said, "I'll take you away and put someone in your seat who looks just like you. Let's go to the beach!" At the beach, Lindsey and Guy played in the waves and collected seashells.

Soon Lindsey's dad was going to pick her up at school. Guy unfurled his wings and flew her back. At school, Guy lay down outside and waited for Lindsey. Then they walked home together. Lindsey studied hard for her math test. The next day she got an A+.

At last it's time to show others your work. Here are some ideas for how you can publish your tale.

Campfire Tale-a-thon ▶

Get together with classmates who have their own tall tales. Then sit in a circle around a make-believe campfire and read your tales out loud.

◀ Be a Cartoonist

Create a storyboard about your special hero. Use posterboard frames to create scenes for the beginning, middle, and end of your hero's adventure. Put dialogue in speech balloons, like those in a comic strip. Use humor and exaggeration in your drawings as well as in your dialogue.

Lights, Camera, Action ▶

Turn your tale into a play. Get classmates to play the parts. (You'll probably want to play the hero yourself!) Make costumes and scenery and entertain other classes with your tale.

Writing a Play Scene

You are in a theater. The lights go dim, the actors come out, and the play begins. Plays are exciting for the audience, the actors, and especially the writer.

A **play** is a story meant to be acted out for an audience. A play begins with a list of the characters and a description of the setting. The story is divided into long parts called acts and shorter parts called scenes. Each line begins with the name of the character who is speaking. Sometimes directions are added to tell the actor what to do.

Meet the Writer

Writer Joseph Robinette chose E. B. White's famous book *Charlotte's Web* to rewrite as a play. In this scene, a young pig named Wilbur learns the reason why the farmer gives him so much food.

PLAYS CHILDREN LOVE

VOLUME II

A treasury of contemporary and classic plays for children

INCLUDES:
CHARLOTTE'S WEB
THE BEST CHRISTMAS PAGEANT EVER
THE WIZARD OF OZ
TREASURE ISLAND
JIM THORPE, ALL-AMERICAN

EDITED BY
COLEMAN A. JENNINGS and AURAND HARRIS
FOREWORD BY CAROL CHANNING

Charlotte's Web

Characters and setting

CHARACTERS

Templeton: A rat   **Wilbur:** A pig
Sheep: A sheep   **Charlotte:** A spider

TIME
The present

SETTING
A barn

Character's name and dialogue

Templeton: By the way, Wilbur, I overheard the Zuckermans talking about all the weight you're putting on. They're very happy.

Wilbur: Good.

Sheep: You know why they're happy, don't you?

Wilbur: You asked me that once before, but you didn't tell me why.

Charlotte: Now, now, old sheep.

Sheep: He has to know sometime.

Wilbur: Know what?

Talk About the Model

As a Reader

★ How do you learn about the characters—who they are and what they are like?

★ Why would you want to act out this scene?

As a Writer

★ How does the writer bring the characters to life?

★ How does the writer control what happens on the stage?

Sheep: Wilbur, I don't like to spread bad news. But they're fattening you up because they're going to kill you.

Wilbur: *(Dismayed)* They're going to what?

Sheep: Kill you. Turn you into old smoked bacon and ham. It'll happen when the weather turns cold. It's a regular conspiracy.

Wilbur: Stop! I don't want to die. I want to stay with all my friends. I want to breathe the beautiful air and lie in the beautiful sun.

Sheep: You're certainly making a beautiful noise. If you don't mind, I think I'll go outside where it's quieter. *(He exits.)*

Wilbur: But I don't want to die.

Charlotte: Wilbur, quiet down. *(A beat as Wilbur tries to control himself.)* You shall not die.

Wilbur: What? Who's going to save me?

Charlotte: I am.

Wilbur: How?

Charlotte: That remains to be seen.

The main problem in the scene is introduced.

The writer's dramatic voice makes the dialogue sound like real speech.

Stage directions tell the actors how to move, speak, and act.

A solution to the problem begins.

Make a Plan

Choose a favorite story that you would like to turn into a play. Make sure that there are at least two characters and something for them to do, such as solve a problem or defeat a villain.

Select the Main Parts for Your Play

To get started, you need to decide if you will use a part of a favorite story, such as a chapter in a book, or all of a short story. Identify these parts for your play.

- the characters
- the setting and time for the action
- the problem the characters must face

Choose What Happens to Your Characters

The characters in your play will be busy solving the problem. You must decide what action each character will take, what each character will say, and what each character will do in your play scene.

Organize Your Play

A chart is one way to organize your play. Don't write everything. Just list the main details.

> **Writer's Tip**
> Use your plan only as a guide. Let your characters' words and actions keep your scene going.

Planning a Play Scene

Story I will use: _____

Main characters: _____

Other characters: _____

Setting: _____

Problem: _____

Main Action: _____

Write It Down

Before you begin to write your play scene, look over the scene from *Charlotte's Web* one more time to recall how to set up your play. Use the model as a guide for your own writing.

Begin Your Play Scene

- List the characters and the setting.
- Introduce the characters and tell the problem.
- Remember to write the name of each speaker before what he or she says.

Keep the Action Going

- Show how the characters try to solve the problem.
- Use the characters' words and actions to show what happens.
- Add stage directions to tell the actors how to speak or move in a special way.

End Your Play

End the scene by showing how everything works out.

Conferencing

Read your play scene aloud with a classmate. Ask your partner if the dialogue sounds like real speech. Ask him or her if the actions are clear from beginning to end.

Look It Over

Reread your scene to yourself. Does the dialogue tell what's happening? Are your stage directions inside parentheses to set them apart?

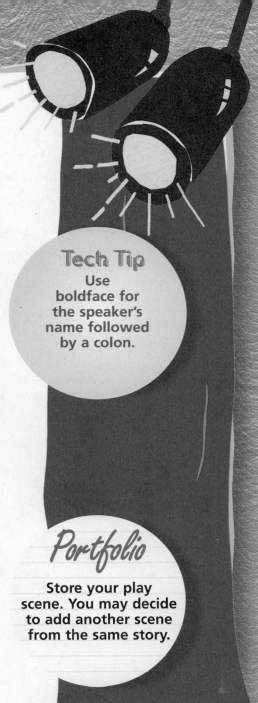

Tech Tip
Use boldface for the speaker's name followed by a colon.

Portfolio
Store your play scene. You may decide to add another scene from the same story.

Writing a Story From History

Meet the Writer

Someday I want to be a newspaper reporter. That's why I chose to write about Nellie Bly, who was one of the first reporters to go undercover.

Dennis Underwood, Louisiana

For years, people have dreamed of time machines that could take them back to great moments in history. Imagine traveling back to see the first astronauts step onto the moon or to watch the pyramids being built.

Writing can create a time machine. A **story from history** is based on a person or an event from history. Parts of the story are real, and other parts can be imagined. Dennis Underwood wrote a story about a real person. He imagined what it would have been like to know Nellie Bly and to write about her in his story.

UNDERCOVER WITH NELLIE BLY

by Dennis Underwood

It was a cold, rainy day in Pittsburgh. A ten-year-old boy stood in a doorway. He was looking for a job instead of being in school. His family was poor, so he had to work. In 1888 there were no laws to keep children in school.

A woman stopped and said, "Young man, why aren't you in school?" The boy said he was looking for a job. He saw that the lady had ink on her hands.

"I have a job for you!" the lady said. She told the boy her name was Nellie Bly. She was a newspaper reporter. Nellie was famous because she would often take a job in a factory so that she could spy. Then she would write stories about how badly the workers were treated.

> The fact is accurate for the time period.

> This character is a real person from history.

> A fact about the person from history

Talk About the Model

As a Reader

★ What details made this time in history come alive?

★ What parts, do you think, are based on facts? Which are imagined?

As a Writer

★ How can you tell that the writer knows a lot about the person from history?

★ Do you think the writer created a believable problem for the story? Why or why not?

Nellie asked the boy, "Will you take a job in a factory where the boss is known to be very mean, especially to children? It could be dangerous!" The boy said yes and was hired in a factory that made wire. He agreed to give Nellie an interview after a few days of working there.

The problem is real for the time period.

The first day on the job the boy learned how mean the boss was. The factory was cold and dark because of no heat and little lighting. Rats ran through the place. The work days were long, and the pay was little. The wire cut the hands of the workers, but they were not allowed to stop for a break.

Descriptive details catch the reader's attention.

The boy told Nellie all the information she wanted to know. Her story hit the newspaper that week. Readers became angry and made the factory owner improve the working conditions. Once again, Nellie Bly had made a difference.

The story ends with a solution to the problem.

Make a Plan

What time in history would you want to visit? Is there a famous person from history who interests you or an event you would like to experience?

Choose a Subject

- Brainstorm names of people and events from history.
- Choose a real person or event for your story.
- Create other characters who meet your real person from history.

Collect Information

- Collect facts and details from books and encyclopedias or get information from history Web sites.
- Write notes on index cards. The more details you collect, the more your story, setting, and characters will seem real to your readers.
- Organize your notes with facts about your person or event from history and facts about the time period.

Writer's Tip
One way to take notes is to ask yourself questions you want to have answered: Who was Nellie Bly?

1883 Factories

1. Many items made by hand

2. Poor heating and lighting

3. Low pay and no breaks

4. Dangerous working conditions

Nellie Bly,   1867–1922

1. Real name: Elizabeth Cochrane Seaman

2. She was born in Pennsylvania.

3. American journalist

4. She worked as a reporter for the Pittsburgh Dispatch, New York World, and New York Journal.

Identify Your Story Parts

- Think about how you will describe this person and time in history.
- Identify a problem that is believable for the time period.
- Think about the events of your story in a logical order. An organizer like this will help you plan.

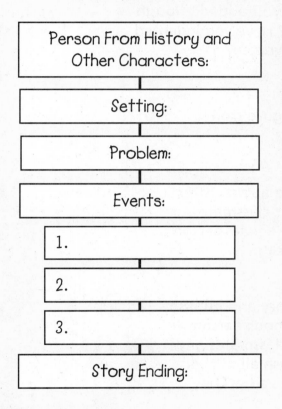

Person From History and Other Characters:

Setting:

Problem:

Events:

1.

2.

3.

Story Ending:

Write It Down

Write Your Story From History

- Imagine a good opening scene to catch your readers' attention. It can be an action, a conversation, or a description.
- Use details from your notes and organizer to make people, places, and things seem real.
- Keep the dialogue true to life. (Remember, George Washington wouldn't have said, "Yeah, man" or "Hey, dude.")
- Tell how the event ended or what happened to your character.

Portfolio

Store your notes and drafts. They might come in handy if you choose to publish your story.

Conferencing

Tell a classmate why this person or event in history interests you. Read your story to your classmate. Ask if your partner thinks your character or event from history seems believable.

Look It Over

Read your story again. Have you added enough details about the time period? Have you indented each new paragraph you've written?

Share Your Work

Now it's time to bring your figure from history to life for your readers.

Role-Play

Dress as the person you wrote about. After reading your story, invite your classmates to interview you. Try to speak like your person from history would have spoken.

Headline News

Create a headline for your story and publish it as an article about your famous person or event. Make copies for your classmates and family. You may want to publish all of the class stories together to create a back-in-time newspaper.

Tech Tip

Run a spell check before you print. Check your story, line by line, for errors your Spelling tool might have missed.

IMAGINE THAT

Writing to Describe

Writing a Descriptive Paragraph

Meet the Writer

Not too many cats are famous for the way they smell, but my cat, Pigeon, is one of a kind. You'll see why!

Rafaela Izquierdo
New Mexico

Click! Click! Do you like to snap photos to keep in an album to remind you of special memories? A **descriptive paragraph** is like a photo album because it tells with words what people, places, or things are like. When you write a descriptive paragraph, you include details that tell how your subject looks, sounds, smells, feels, or tastes. In "My Pigeon," Rafaela uses colorful words to paint a perfect picture of her cat. The writer's words let you see, hear, feel, and even smell her cat.

My Pigeon
by Rafaela Izquierdo

Pigeon is a special cat for many reasons. He is a big fuzzy orange cat with glowing green eyes and is the bossiest cat in America. If his food dish is empty, Pigeon follows me around and complains in loud meows. He purrs like a truck engine when I give him food. He eats as if he is starving, but he isn't! He is about as huge as a watermelon. When my mom puts on perfume, he leaps onto her lap and won't jump off until he gets some on him, too! Then he rolls on the ground and gets dust all over him. Pigeon is the only cat I know who looks like a dust mop and smells like flowers.

IMAGINE THAT

Writing to Describe

Writing a Descriptive Paragraph

Meet the Writer

Not too many cats are famous for the way they smell, but my cat, Pigeon, is one of a kind. You'll see why!

Rafaela Izquierdo
New Mexico

Click! Click! Do you like to snap photos to keep in an album to remind you of special memories? A **descriptive paragraph** is like a photo album because it tells with words what people, places, or things are like. When you write a descriptive paragraph, you include details that tell how your subject looks, sounds, smells, feels, or tastes. In "My Pigeon," Rafaela uses colorful words to paint a perfect picture of her cat. The writer's words let you see, hear, feel, and even smell her cat.

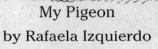

My Pigeon
by Rafaela Izquierdo

Pigeon is a special cat for many reasons. He is a big fuzzy orange cat with glowing green eyes and is the bossiest cat in America. If his food dish is empty, Pigeon follows me around and complains in loud meows. He purrs like a truck engine when I give him food. He eats as if he is starving, but he isn't! He is about as huge as a watermelon. When my mom puts on perfume, he leaps onto her lap and won't jump off until he gets some on him, too! Then he rolls on the ground and gets dust all over him. Pigeon is the only cat I know who looks like a dust mop and smells like flowers.

Talk About the Model

★ How does the writer let you know what the paragraph is about?

★ What details does the writer include to make her cat seem real?

★ What words help you see, hear, feel, and smell the cat?

Make a Plan

- Choose a person, place, or thing you'd like to describe.
- Jot down words that tell how your subject *looks, feels, sounds, smells,* or *tastes.* These are called sensory words.
- Think about your audience. Will they know about your subject, or will it be something completely new to them?

Write It Down

Begin your paragraph with a sentence that introduces your topic.

- Use sensory details that help your readers picture your subject in their minds.
- Organize your details so they make sense.
- End with a statement that sums up what your subject is like or how you feel about it.

Conferencing

Read your descriptive paragraph to a partner. Does your partner have a clear picture of your subject? Could you use other words that would give a better picture?

Look It Over

Read your paragraph again. Have you used colorful words to describe your subject? Have you organized your paragraph so it is easy for a reader to follow?

Writer's Tip
You may not be able to use all five senses in your description.

Portfolio
Store your paragraph. After a day, read it again. You may want to add details to improve your description.

Writing an Observation Report

Meet the Writer

Wayne Grover, who lives in Florida, is a conservation activist, scuba diver, whitewater rafter, and hiker.

Whom do you picture making an observation? Do you think of detectives taking notes about someone they're watching or of a scientist working in a laboratory?

An **observation report** is a special description that records the sights, sounds, smells, and feelings the writer observes at a particular time and place. The purpose is to describe the scene so vividly that readers will feel they are there.

Here is a report about a magical moment beneath the sea. It is from the book *Dolphin Adventure: A True Story* by underwater naturalist Wayne Grover.

BEECH TREE CHAPTER BOOKS

Wayne Grover

Dolphin Adventure

A TRUE STORY

I write my books and articles to let people know they can make a difference.

Talk About the Model

As a Reader

★ What vivid details in this passage capture your attention?

★ What feelings about the sea do you get from reading this report?

★ Would you like to visit a time and place like this one? Why or why not?

As a Writer

★ Why did the writer write this report?

★ How does the writer show you what scuba diving is like?

★ How does the writer make you feel part of the experience?

Down, down I went until I was just above the bottom. I leveled off and let the Gulf Stream current gently push me northward along the reef.

The beauty that surrounded me was like a fairyland that morning. Thousands of fish darted about the reef as they too enjoyed the perfect swimming conditions. There were colorful tiny fishes darting in and out of the coral and reef rocks. There were large schools of jacks, yellow-tailed snappers, and grunts moving in unison as if marching to an army sergeant's command.

I saw a school of barracudas flashing by like a hundred sharp, shiny sea knives as they tried to run down their breakfast. Beneath my feet, two stingrays scurried along the sea bottom, flapping their big wings like giant bats of the deep. It was nature on parade.

The report is organized in paragraphs.

The description begins at the moment the writer arrives on the scene.

The writer names details in the order that he sees them.

An unusual sight is compared with something more familiar.

Make a Plan

It's time for you to be the observer.

Choose a Time and Place

Choose a location that interests you. It can be at home, in school, on a playing field, or in your community. Choose a time to observe, such as during science class or recess.

Observe and Take Notes

Find a comfortable seat and observe. Take notes to record what's happening. Include what you see, hear, and feel. As things happen, write as many details as you can. You can draw a sketch of what you observe.

Write It Down

Now it's time to write a report to describe what you saw, heard, and learned.

Organize Your Thoughts

One way to organize your report is to tell about events, moment by moment, in the order in which you observed them. You can also organize your observations around one main idea and include details.

Include Sensory Details

You want your readers to experience what you saw. To do this, include details to tell readers what you saw, heard, felt, and even smelled.

Tech Tip
Use the Tab key to indent the first line of each paragraph.

Conferencing

Read your report to a group of classmates. Can they picture exactly what you observed? What details worked best? What can you add to make your description clearer?

Portfolio

Store your draft. You can publish it by itself or you might want to include it as part of a longer description.

Look It Over

Read your observation report. Do your details "show" your readers what you observed? The writer uses the words *gently* and *colorful*. Can you include words that end with *ly* or *ful*?

What a Character!

There is an old saying that goes, "No two people are alike." A character sketch is a writer's chance to prove that this is true.

Like a good photograph, a **character sketch** captures how a person looks, dresses, and acts. But a character sketch goes further. It also tells readers about the subject's personality, habits, likes, dislikes, and so on. The writer of a character sketch wants to capture in words what makes a person or that character special.

Meet the Writer

I wrote about my sister's boyfriend, Jake. I thought he would be great to write about because he does cool things. For instance, he is making a movie!

Raymund Villanueva
Texas

A Character Sketch

★ **Tells about a real or imagined person**

★ **Gives details about how the person looks and acts**

★ **Describes the character's personality, likes, and dislikes**

★ **Uses colorful words to make the person seem real**

★ **Tells how the writer feels about the character**

Think It Through

Choosing a character to describe is your first task. Your character can be a real person you know, an imagined person, or a character from a book.

Brainstorming

To find the character you want to write about, brainstorm by writing a list of names on paper.

> List the names of characters you might write about. Make one list of real people you know. In a second list, write the names of imagined characters or characters from books you have read.

Select a Topic

Raymund chose to write about his sister's boyfriend, Jake Taylor, because he is an interesting person. Read over your list of possible characters.

- Which character do you find the most interesting?
- Which character would your audience be most interested in hearing about?

Choose the subject for your character sketch. Circle the character's name on your list.

Raymund's List

Real people:
Uncle Carlos
Jake Taylor
My mom

Imagined characters:
A boy in a wagon train
James Henry Trotter from the book James and the Giant Peach

Design a Plan

Raymund wrote a list of questions to plan what he needed to find out about his character, Jake. Then Raymund spent time with Jake to observe him and get answers to his questions. Raymund also talked with people who know Jake. Raymund wrote the details he learned as each question was answered.

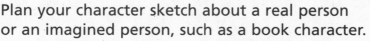

Who is my character?	Jake Taylor
How old is he?	16
What does he look like?	short brown hair parted in the middle, light green eyes, 5 feet 8 inches tall, wears blue jeans, likes shirts with logos
Where does he go to school?	Travis High, tenth grade
What are his favorite things?	playing drums, making movies, and collecting books, comics, and old movies

Plan your character sketch about a real person or an imagined person, such as a book character.

- Write questions you want answered about your character.
- Find answers about imagined characters in books. If your subject is a real person, spend time with him or her. Talk with people who know your subject well.
- Write your answer next to each question.

Conferencing

Share your questions and answers with a partner. Ask if the details give a clear picture of your subject. Does your partner have any questions you should include?

Portfolio

You'll be gathering plenty of information. Keep everything in your portfolio so nothing gets lost.

Put It Into Words

Raymund collected interesting information to include in his character sketch. Do his details give a good picture of Jake? Do you know anyone like him?

A Normal Teen
by Raymund Villanueva

The beginning introduces and describes the character.

Jake Taylor is a really cool guy. Jennifer, my big sister, is his girlfriend. Jake is 5 feet 8 inches tall. His eyes are light green. He has short brown hair, which he parts in the middle. He usaully wears blue jeans and shirts with logos on them.

The writer lets the readers know the character is a real person.

He studies hard to get good grades. Jake is 16 years old and in the tenth grade at Travis High School. He thinks an education is important for everyone.

Details describe the character's interests.

A collection of superhero comics and old movies are Jakes favorite things. He sometimes plays drums in a band, but he plans to be a movie director some day. Right now he's making a horror movie called <u>the creature</u>. He's good at telling his friends just how to act.

The writer shares his opinion of the character.

I see him driving a red sports car in hollywood some day. When he's famous, I'll feel proud to say that I know this very cool guy.

As you write your draft, ask yourself
★ **Subject:**   Who is the character I am describing?
★ **Audience:**   Who will read about my character?
★ **Purpose:**   What details will help my readers see my character as I do?
★ **Form:**   What details should I include in each paragraph of my character sketch?

As you write your character sketch, keep your prewriting questions and answers handy. Remember that your purpose is to use words to bring your character to life for your readers. Use this Drafting Checklist as a guide.

Drafting Checklist

• Introduce your character and use details to describe him or her.

• Let your readers know if your character is real or imagined.

• Use vivid action words to show how the person acts and what he or she does.

• Organize your details so that your character sketch is easy to follow.

• Use the ending to sum up who your character is and how you feel about him or her.

Conferencing

Read your character sketch to a classmate. Can your partner describe your character to you? Are there any important details you can add?

Writer's Tip
Include facts and opinions about your character to make your sketch interesting.

Tech Tip
Choose a type size and font to match your character's personality.

Take Another Look

Raymund included plenty of facts and colorful details in his first draft. He decided to work on the organization a bit. What changes did he make? How do the changes improve his description?

A Normal Teen

by Raymund Villanueva

~~Jake Taylor is just a normal teenager—or is he?~~

○Jake Taylor is a really cool guy. Jennifer, my big sister, is

and
his girlfriend. Jake is 5 feet 8 inches tall. His eyes are light green.

He has short brown hair, which he parts in the middle.

He likes to wear dark glasses like a movie star.

He usually wears blue jeans and shirts with logos on them.

He studies hard to get good grades. Jake is 16 years old and

in the tenth grade at Travis High School. He thinks an

education is important for everyone.

A collection of superhero comics and old movies are Jakes

favorite things. He sometimes plays drums in a band, but he

plans to be a movie director some day. Right now he's making

He has a lot of imagination, and
a horror movie called the creature. He's good at telling his

friends just how to act.

Jake will be successful because he works hard.

I see him driving a red sports car in hollywood some

day. When he's famous, I'll feel proud to say that I know this

very cool guy.

The beginning is changed to add interest.

Two short, choppy sentences are combined.

An added detail describes the character's personality.

A sentence is moved for better organization.

A sentence is expanded.

The writer adds another opinion.

Read your character sketch. Does it give a clear picture of the person you are writing about? Can you see ways to improve your description? This Revising Checklist will help you.

Revising Marks

≡	capitalize
∧	add ·
◡	remove
⊙	add a period
/	make lowercase
◯	move
∿	transpose

Revising Checklist

- Does your beginning sentence catch your readers' interest and introduce the character in a clear and interesting way?
- Does your description draw a complete and colorful picture of the character?
- Can you improve your sketch by adding more details or expanding sentences?
- Should anything be cut or moved to make your writing easier to follow?
- Do you end with one final thought about your character?

Conferencing

Read your character sketch to a classmate. Use the Revising Checklist to talk about changes you might make to improve your sketch.

Writer's Tip
Keep your book open to the revising marks and learn to use them while you are revising.

Portfolio
Store your draft in your portfolio. If your character is a real person, share your draft with your subject.

Become a Super Writer

Check your writing for short, choppy sentences. Improve them by combining short sentences or by adding adjectives or adverbs. For help with combining sentences, see page 227 in the *Writer's Handbook* section.

Polish Your Writing

Raymund revised his character sketch of Jake several times. When he finally was happy with it, he was ready to check for mistakes in grammar and spelling. What did he find?

Add a comma in a compound sentence.

Transpose letters to correct the spelling of a word.

Add an apostrophe to form a possessive noun.

Capitalize a title.

Indent a paragraph.

Capitalize a place name.

A Normal Teen
by Raymund Villanueva

Jake Taylor is just a normal teenager–or is he? Jennifer, my big sister, is his girlfriend. Jake is 5 feet 8 inches tall and his eyes are light green. He has short brown hair, which he parts in the middle. He likes to wear dark glasses like a movie star.

He usually wears blue jeans and shirts with logos on them.

Jake is 16 years old and in the tenth grade at Travis High School. He studies hard to get good grades. He thinks an education is important for everyone.

A collection of superhero comics and old movies are Jakes favorite things. He sometimes plays drums in a band, but he plans to be a movie director some day. Right now he's making a horror movie called the creature. He has a lot of imagination, and he's good at telling his friends just how to act.

Jake will be successful because he works hard. I see him driving a red sports car in hollywood some day. When he's famous, I'll feel proud to say that I know this very cool guy.

Artists usually touch up a sketch or portrait just before they finish. Now it's time to get your character sketch just right by proofreading for spelling and grammar mistakes. Use this Editing and Proofreading Checklist to help you.

Editing and Proofreading Checklist

- Did I spell all words correctly?

  See page 259 in the **Writer's Handbook** *section.*

- Is the first line of each paragraph indented?

  See page 251 in the **Writer's Handbook** *section.*

- Have I used apostrophes to show possessive forms of nouns?

  See page 231 in the **Writer's Handbook** *section.*

- Are titles and proper names capitalized?

  See page 229 in the **Writer's Handbook** *section.*

Proofreading Marks

¶	indent first line of paragraph
≡	capitalize
∧ or ∨	add
℘	remove
⊙	add a period
/	make lowercase
○	spelling mistake
∽	move
∾	transpose

Tech Tip

If you are using a computer, instead of underlining titles put them in italics. That's what professional writers do.

Conferencing

Ask a classmate to check your changes with you. As you edit and proofread together, does your partner find any other corrections to be made?

Become a Super Writer

When you write about your character, show ownership by using a possessive form of a noun (*Jake's*) or a possessive pronoun (*his*). For help with possessive forms, see pages 231 and 243 in the *Writer's Handbook* section.

Portfolio

When you've polished your sketch, look back at your first draft. See the progress you've made!

Share Your Work

Raymund did a great job with his sketch. Even Jake thought it was great. Raymund read his sketch to a friend who never met Jake. Raymund asked his friend to draw a picture of Jake based on the character sketch.

A Normal Teen
by Raymund Villanueva

Jake Taylor is just a normal teenager—or is he? Jennifer, my big sister, is his girlfriend. Jake is 5 feet 8 inches tall, and his eyes are light green. He has short brown hair, which he parts in the middle. He likes to wear dark glasses like a movie star. He usually wears blue jeans and shirts with logos on them.

Jake is 16 years old and in the tenth grade at Travis High School. He studies hard to get good grades. He thinks an education is important for everyone.

A collection of superhero comics and old movies are Jake's favorite things. He sometimes plays drums in a band, but he plans to be a movie director some day. Right now he's making a horror movie called <u>The Creature</u>. He has a lot of imagination, and he's good at telling his friends just how to act.

Jake will be successful because he works hard. I see him driving a red sports car in Hollywood some day. When he's famous, I'll be able to say that I know this really cool guy.

Now it's time to show off your character. Here are some ideas about how you might publish your writing.

Sketch Artist ▶

How will a classmate picture the character you have described? This is one way to find out.

- Read your character sketch to a partner.
- Ask your partner to draw a picture of the person you have described.
- See how close your partner comes to drawing your character as you see him or her.

◀ Mystery Person

If you've written about a classmate or a person your classmates know, make a game of "Who is the mystery person?" Read your sketch to your class, but leave out the names. See if they can guess the person you have described.

A Great Gift Idea ▶

Create a cover for your character sketch by drawing a picture of your real or imagined person and attaching it to your finished piece. If your character is a real person you know, present your finished work to your subject. If your character is from a book, display your writing in the school library for others to read.

Writing a Compare-and-Contrast Description

Meet the Writer

I used to live in Chicago, but last year my family moved. Now I live in a farmhouse in Ohio. Talk about changing your life! Here's the inside story of what it's like.

Veronica Chang
Ohio

Do you like to solve picture puzzles that ask you to find the one picture that doesn't belong? To do this, you compare to see how the pictures are alike and contrast to find how they are different.

In writing, a **compare-and-contrast description** tells about two subjects by describing how they are alike and different. When Veronica Chang moved from the city to the country, she discovered how two different places can be alike in many ways, so she wrote to tell about it.

The first paragraph identifies the two subjects.

City and Country
by Veronica Chang

When I told my friends I was going to move from Chicago to Ohio, they couldn't believe it. I was worried because I'd never been out of the city before, except on vacation trips. Would life be very different from Chicago? Well, see for yourself.

Many things are different about the city and country. In Chicago we lived in a tall brick apartment building close to large stores and Lake Michigan. Our building was filled with people, but I only knew a few of them. At night I could see the shining lights of the city. Now we live in an old farmhouse on three acres of land. Our nearest neighbors are half a mile away. All the people are friendly and came to greet us with loads of food. At night it's dark for miles, and all I hear are crickets!

Details tell how the two subjects are different.

Talk About the Model

★ What details tell you about the writer's life in Chicago? in Ohio?

★ How does the writer convince you that some parts of life in the city and country are the same and others are different?

★ After you read the final paragraph, what feelings about city and country life does the writer leave you with?

Some things about life in the country and city are the same. In Chicago my mom and I loved to go shopping together. Here in the country we go on all-day shopping sprees in country stores and farmers' markets. The greatest thing that's the same is the kids. We like a lot of the same music. We laugh at the same jokes and TV shows, and we see the same movies that city kids see. I also found a soccer team to play on. Best of all, I found a good friend to spend time with— just like back in Chicago.

When I think about the most important things, like family and friends, maybe there aren't so many differences between the city and the country. Personally, I think they're both great.

Details tell how the two subjects are the same.

The end summarizes the likenesses and differences and expresses the writer's opinion.

Make a Plan

Before you write your compare-and-contrast description, you must decide which two subjects you will compare and contrast.

Select Interesting Subjects

- Jot down pairs of subjects you can compare and contrast: places, people, objects, sports, or animals.

- Choose subjects you know about or are interested in.

- Make sure the subjects are alike and different in important ways.

Use a Venn Diagram to Show Likenesses and Differences

- Make a list of details about each subject. Write down all the ideas you can think of.

- Once you have all your ideas, organize them in a Venn diagram. In the middle, put details about how the two subjects are alike. In the other parts of each circle, list the differences.

Here's the diagram Veronica made to plan what she would write about the city and the country.

City Life

lots of neighbors

didn't know many neighbors

big apartment building

bright and noisy nights

shop with Mom

kids like same music, jokes, TV shows, and movies

a good friend

soccer team

Country Life

neighbors are spread out

met the neighbors

old farmhouse

dark and quiet nights

Organize Your Description

Once you have the details about your two subjects, plan how you will organize them as your description. A compare-and-contrast description has four paragraphs. You may want to make a chart like this to jot down notes to show what you will include in each paragraph.

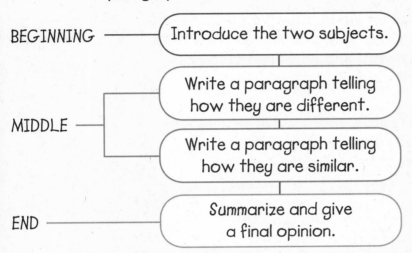

BEGINNING — Introduce the two subjects.

MIDDLE —
Write a paragraph telling how they are different.

Write a paragraph telling how they are similar.

END — Summarize and give a final opinion.

Write It Down

Once you have organized your ideas, you are ready to write your compare-and-contrast description.

Introduce Your Subjects

- Write an opening paragraph to introduce your two subjects.
- Identify your subjects in an interesting way.

Present Your Facts

- Write a paragraph that tells how the two subjects are different. Use details from your Venn diagram.
- Write another paragraph to tell how your two subjects are alike. Use details from the center of your Venn diagram.

Sum Up Your Ideas

- End by summing up likenesses and differences.
- Give your opinion about whether your subjects are mostly alike or different.

Conferencing

Read your description to a classmate. Ask your partner to find the ways in which the things are alike and different. Are your details clear? If not, choose new details or reorganize your description.

Look It Over

Read your description again. Have you included plenty of details to tell how your subjects are alike and different? Can you add adjectives with *er* or *est* to make comparisons?

Share Your Work

If you decide to publish your description, here are some ideas for you to try.

Mail It

Veronica found an interesting way to publish her description. First, she shared it with her new friends in Ohio. Then, she made copies and mailed them to her friends back in Chicago. Everyone was surprised to find out that the two places were not so different after all.

Create an Album

Make a compare-and-contrast album. Create two sections, one for each of the things you are comparing and contrasting. Fill each section with photos or drawings that show the details you are describing. Put your written description on the first page.

You're a Poet

Do you have a favorite poem that you like to recite? What makes this poem so special that it will always be stuck in your memory? A **poem** is a colorful word picture about something the writer has seen, thought, or felt. In a poem, every word counts. Every word helps to create a certain mood to make the reader feel what the writer feels.

Free verse is one kind of poetry. In free-verse poetry, the writer describes something in an imaginative way. There is no special form.

Words are arranged so that ideas stand out. Free-verse poetry can rhyme, but it doesn't have to. Imagination is the only limit!

A Free-Verse Poem

★ **Describes a subject in an imaginative or unusual way**

★ **Uses words in a colorful way to express a mood and tell what the writer has seen, thought, or felt**

★ **Uses imagination, rhythm, and sometimes rhyme to create a form for the poem**

★ **Often makes comparisons with the words *like* or *as* to describe the subject**

Meet the Writer

My poem describes a moment when I was outside one night. I was watching moonlight shining on the water. Then a dragonfly came along and distracted me.

Kim Mathews
Virginia

Think It Through

For your free-verse poem, think of a great topic that you can describe in an unusual or imaginative way. Your topic might be a special place, a friend, a pet, favorite music, or an experience you want to describe for others.

Brainstorming

One way to brainstorm topics for a poem is to think back over the past few months about the experiences you have had. What experiences bring back strong feelings and wonderful memories?

> Make a list like Kim's. Write down ideas that have a special meaning for you. There is no "right" or "wrong" idea for a poem.

Your Turn

Kim's List
nighttime at the pond
playing the drums
exploring the beach
camping with my
best friend

Select a Topic

Look at your list of ideas. Choose the best idea for the topic of your free-verse poem.

• Which idea do you want to explore further?
• Which idea has the most meaning for you?
• Which topic would you want to share with others?

Design a Plan

Once you have chosen a topic for your poem, think of colorful words that tell about it. Since Kim enjoys the peace and quiet of nighttime at the pond, she chose that as her subject. She wrote down any idea that came to mind and ended up with this cluster.

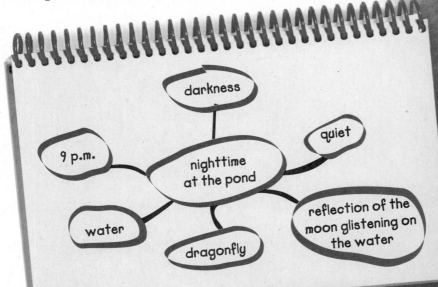

Choose your topic and create your own word cluster as a plan for writing your poem.

- Write your topic in the middle of a piece of paper.
- Make a cluster by writing words that tell what you see, hear, and feel.
- Add mood-setting words to your list. For example, if your poem will be funny, add funny words, such as *clodhopper*, *loony*, *snort*.

Conferencing

Share your word cluster with a classmate. Can your partner picture the topic you have chosen for your poem? Do your partner's questions or suggestions help you think of other ideas to add to your cluster?

Portfolio

Keep your plan in your portfolio. You may want to add words to your cluster that come to you during the day.

Drafting

Put It Into Words

Here's the first draft of Kim's free-verse poem. She decided to write her poem to share a nighttime experience with her readers. Kim chose the form for her poem. She also tried to capture a certain mood or feeling. What feeling do you get from reading Kim's poem?

Free to Fly
by Kim Mathews

The writer describes the time and place of her experience.

Sitting at the pond at 9 P.M.

A comparison called a *simile* tells what the scene looks like.

All was dark as ink and still as a photograph,

except the moon's reflection glistened in the water.

Suddenly I saw a dragonfly overhead.

It hit the water, destroying the golden image.

The mood or feeling changes.

I felt a chill down my back.

I reached up to catch it.

I tried once. I missed. I tried twice. I missed.

A new feeling is expressed.

On my third try I caught it.

Then, feeling giulty, I let it go.

It flown away, and took my peaceful moment with it!

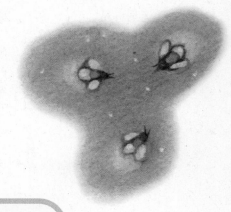

Think Like a Writer

As you write your free-verse poem, ask yourself

★ What vivid words can I use to bring my subject to life?

★ How can I arrange my words so that certain words and ideas stand out?

★ Will I paint a word picture with my poem? Will I tell a story?

It's time to begin writing your free-verse poem. Use ideas from your cluster. Don't worry about the form. Just think about the feeling you want to express. Here is a Drafting Checklist to use.

Drafting Checklist

- Get your readers' attention with the first line.
- Use words that express a certain mood or feeling to describe your subject.
- Describe things by making comparisons called similes, which use the words *like* or *as*.
- Be brief. Remember, every word counts in a poem.
- Create your own form for your poem.

Tech Tip
The Return key will help you experiment with line lengths. Try ending lines in a few different places to see which works best.

Writer's Tip
Leave wide margins so you will have room to add details and colorful words.

Conferencing

Read your poem to a partner. Can your partner describe the mood you want your poem to create? Is the meaning of your poem clear?

Portfolio
Store your word cluster and draft in your portfolio.

Take Another Look

Kim thought her first draft had a lot of good ideas for a free-verse poem, but she wanted to make some changes. How do they make her poem better?

Free to Fly
by Kim Mathews

Sitting at the pond at 9 P.M.

Change a word. · ➤ picture

All was dark as ink and still as a ~~photograph,~~
⌃

except the moon's reflection glistened in the water.

Suddenly I saw a dragonfly overhead.

Add a sound word. · · · · · · · · · · · ➤ plink,

It hit the water, destroying the golden image.
⌃

I felt a chill down my back.

Make line breaks to create a stronger rhythm. · · ➤

I reached up to catch it.

➤ I tried once. ⟨I missed.⟩ ⟨I tried twice,⟩ ⟨I missed.⟩

Replace a word with a better action word. · · · · · · · · · · · · · · ➤ escape

On my third try I caught it.

Then, feeling giulty, I let it ~~go.~~
⌃

It flown away, and took my peaceful moment with it!

Read your poem aloud. Do your words create the picture you want your reader to see? Can you rearrange words so that certain ideas stand out? Can you use comparisons to describe something more clearly? Use this Revising Checklist to help you find other things to think about.

Revising Checklist

- Do you use vivid, colorful words and words with pleasing sounds to describe a person, place, or thing?
- Do you use the words *like* or *as* to make comparisons called similes?
- Does every detail help to set the mood? Are there extra words that you don't need?
- Does your poem have the rhythm you want? Do you want to include any words that rhyme?

Conferencing

Read your free-verse poem to a classmate. Talk with your partner about the questions in the Revising Checklist. Think about ways to improve your poem.

Revising Marks

- ≡ capitalize
- ^ add
- remove
- ⊙ add a period
- / make lowercase
- move
- transpose

Writer's Tip
Read your poem aloud as you write. Make line breaks that sound natural to you.

Portfolio
Clip together all your notes and drafts. You might want to rethink a change you have made.

Become a Super Writer

Your poem should be pleasing to the ear. Try including sound words in your poem. For help with onomatopoeia, see the *Writer's Handbook* section, on page 213.

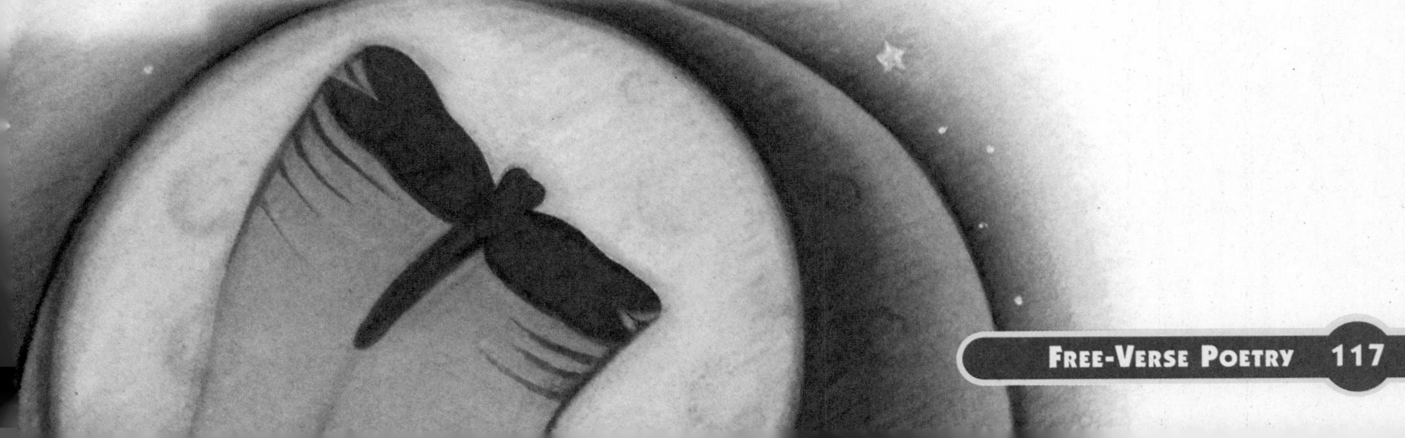

Polish Your Writing

Kim read her revised poem and got excited! She really thought the changes made it better. It was time for one last round of polishing. What corrections did she make to get ready to publish her poem?

Free to Fly
by Kim Mathews

Words are added to make a sentence complete.

I was
Sitting at the pond at 9 P.M.

All was dark as ink and still as a picture,

An ending is changed from ed to ing.

glistening
except the moon's reflection glistened in the water.

Suddenly I saw a dragonfly overhead.

It hit the water, plink, destroying the golden image.

I felt a chill down my back.

I reached up to catch it.

I tried once.

I missed.

A comma is added to make the rhythm stronger.

I tried twice.

I missed.

On my third try, I caught it.

A misspelled word is corrected.

guilty
Then, feeling giulty, I let it escape.

A verb form is changed.

flew
It flown away, and took my peaceful moment with it!

Now it's time to polish your free-verse poem. Read your poem aloud. Keep looking for errors in spelling and grammar. Use this Editing and Proofreading Checklist to help you.

Proofreading Marks

¶	indent first line of paragraph
≡	capitalize
∧ or ∨	add
ᴓ	remove
⊙	add a period
/	make lowercase
◯	spelling mistake
◯	move
∼	transpose

Editing and Proofreading Checklist

- Do I use a comma to separate a phrase from the rest of the sentence?
  See page 255 in the **Writer's Handbook** section.

- Do I use periods when I want to end one sentence and begin another?
  See the **Writer's Handbook** section, page 251.

- Do I want to change any word form by adding a different ending?
  See the **Writer's Handbook** section, pages 260–261.

- Have I spelled all the words correctly?
  See the **Writer's Handbook** section, pages 259–268.

Conferencing

Read your poem to a classmate. Show the corrections you have made. Ask your partner to check your poem again. Discuss other corrections you need to make.

Tech Tip
You can use your computer's Scroll feature to look at sections of your poem as you revise.

Portfolio
Clip your final copy to the earlier drafts you've been saving. You've come a long way as a poet!

★ Become a Super Writer

Sometimes you will want to change the ending of a word to tell whether an action happened in the past or is happening now. For help when you spell words with endings, see pages 260–261 in the **Writer's Handbook** section.

Share Your Work

A free-verse poem describes a subject the writer has experienced. The subject is so special that the writer wants to share it with others. Here is Kim's finished free-verse poem. Notice how her words can take you to the pond at 9 P.M. Kim made her poem look magical by publishing it in an exciting frame.

Free to Fly
by Kim Mathews

I was sitting at the pond at 9 P.M.
All was dark as ink and still as a picture,
except the moon's reflection glistening in the water.
Suddenly I saw a dragonfly overhead.
It hit the water, <u>plink</u>, destroying the golden image.
I felt a chill down my back.
I reached up to catch it.
I tried once.
I missed.
I tried twice.
I missed.
On my third try, I caught it.
Then, feeling guilty, I let it escape.
It flew away, and took my peaceful moment with it!

The following suggestions tell some ways you can share your poem with classmates, friends, and family.

Frame It ▶

Make a colorful frame to display the poem you have written.

- Choose a colorful posterboard. Cut a frame from the board.
- Decorate the frame with paint, beads, glitter, twigs, feathers, buttons, or other small items that relate to your poem.
- Hang your framed poem in your classroom or school library.

◀ Set It to Music

Set your poem to music. Think of a melody that fits the rhythm of your words. Then read your poem aloud for classmates while softly playing music.

Picture Your Poem ▶

Draw a colorful picture for your poem. If you wish, you can make the poem part of the picture and experiment with the shape of some of the words you write. Here is a line from Kim's poem that could be written in a different way.

Writing Haiku

Not all poetry is free verse. There are other forms of poetry that are quite popular and are written in a particular way. **Haiku** is one example of a poetry form with a special pattern that writers follow.

Haiku is a form of poetry from Japan. Haiku is often written about nature. The poems are always three lines long and usually have seventeen syllables. Most haiku don't rhyme, and most have no title.

Line 1 = 5 syllables

Line 2 = 7 syllables

Line 3 = 5 syllables

This haiku was written by Kazue Mizumura. The poem is from her book *Flower, Moon, Snow: A Book of Haiku*. Kazue paints a picture of a tiny bird sitting on a frozen branch in wintertime. Read the poem aloud.

Meet the Writer

Kazue Mizumura is a Japanese-born illustrator and writer. She has also done advertising layout and Japanese brush drawing.

Flower Moon Snow
A BOOK OF HAIKU
By Kazue Mizumura

Please bird, don't go yet.
You are the finishing touch.
To the snowy branch.

The form has three lines and seventeen syllables.

A scene in nature is described.

Talk About the Model

As a Reader

★ What do you picture as you read the poem?

★ How does reading haiku aloud help you picture the things described?

As a Writer

★ Why did the poet choose haiku instead of free verse or some other form of poetry?

★ What does the writer have to keep in mind when writing haiku?

Make a Plan

Now it's time for you to write a haiku of your own.

- Pick a subject from nature that is interesting to you. Think about one of these ideas: a season (summer, fall, winter, spring), a creature in the wild (a fawn, bats, baby robins), weather (rainbows, wind, snowflakes).

- List words about your topic that can be used in your haiku.

Write It Down

As you write haiku, use colorful language and details that paint a picture for your reader.

- Get ideas down on paper. Read each line aloud as you write it.

- Choose words that express your feelings about the subject.

- Rewrite your poem, changing or moving words until you get the 5-7-5 syllable pattern.

Conferencing

Read your haiku to a partner. What scene in nature does your partner picture? What feeling does your poem express? Discuss changes you will make.

Look It Over

Read your poem aloud. Does your haiku express the feeling you want expressed? You can change one or two words as long as the syllable count remains the same.

Tech Tip
Keep all the poems you write in one main file.

Writer's Tip
Use a thesaurus to find a variety of word choices to use in your poem.

Portfolio
File away all versions of your haiku with other types of poems you have written.

Writing a Limerick

A **limerick** is a humorous poem written in five lines. Limericks are fun to read, and the subject is usually not very serious. Limericks also have a pattern of beats, or stressed syllables, that create the special rhythm.

Lines 1, 2, and 5 rhyme.

Lines 3 and 4 rhyme.

Lines 1, 2, and 5 have three beats.

Lines 3 and 4 have two beats.

In her limerick, Mary Ann Hoberman features a bookworm with an appetite and a change of heart. The silliness of the subject and the rhyme and rhythm make the limerick fun to read aloud.

As a child, I would sit on a swing in my backyard and make up songs to sing to myself.

Lines 1, 2, and 5 and lines 3 and 4 show a rhyme pattern.

The beats in each line are underlined.

A <u>book</u>worm of <u>cur</u>ious <u>breed</u>
Took a <u>bite</u> of a <u>book</u> out of <u>greed</u>
When he <u>found</u> it was <u>tas</u>ty,
He <u>said</u>, "I've been <u>has</u>ty.
I <u>think</u> I shall <u>learn</u> how to <u>read</u>."

The poem has a humorous, silly theme.

Talk About the Model

As a Reader

★ What makes a limerick fun to read?

★ Do you prefer the quiet beauty of haiku or the catchy, funny rhyme and beat of the limerick? Explain why.

As a Writer

★ How does the writer add humor to her poem?

★ What does the writer have to remember when writing a limerick?

Make a Plan

Now it's time to try your hand at writing a limerick of your own.

- Think of a funny topic. Keep it simple. You have just five lines in which to tell a story.

- Many limericks begin by introducing a character, a person, or an animal. Here are some sample first lines.

> There once was a clown with a frown . . .
>
> There was a coyote out west . . .

- Think of groups of three words that rhyme and also have a humorous feel to them. Below are some examples.

> pool   drool   cruel
> Frankie   hankie   crankie

Tech Tip

To keep track of the rhymes in your limerick, boldface the rhyming words.

Writer's Tip

Keep an ongoing list of rhyming words in your journal to choose from.

Write It Down

Describe your subject by using colorful language. Include details that paint a humorous picture.

- Start off by introducing a person or an animal.
- Say each line to yourself as you write.
- Rewrite your limerick until you have the rhyme pattern and rhythm just right.
- Remember that your limerick is meant to entertain your readers.

Conferencing

Ask a partner to read your limerick. What does your partner like best about your limerick? Is there a way to add humor?

Look It Over

Read your poem aloud. Will different rhyming words make your limerick more entertaining?

Share Your Work

Wouldn't you like to share your poems with others? Here are some suggestions for ways to publish your poetry.

Recite It

Recite your poem for an audience. Use background music, a photograph or slides, or a drawing on an overhead projector to show the subject of your poem.

Submit Your Poem

Many magazines such as *Owl*, *Highlights for Children*, *Stone Soup*, and *Creative Kids* feature student writing. Your parent or teacher can also check out Internet Web sites that publish poetry. Some are Kidzpage, poetry4kids, Positively Poetry, Poetry Post, Poetry Pals, and Kid Lit Poetry Gallery.

Portfolio

Keep all the versions of your limerick in your portfolio. You may like an earlier draft better.

JUST THE FACTS

Writing to Inform

Writing an Informative Paragraph

Meet the Writer

My family lived in Mexico for a year. I saw some amazing pyramids there and decided to share what I learned about one of them.

David Urban
Minnesota

One of the most important things writing can do is to inform. An **informative paragraph** gives information about a subject or explains something in a clear, well-organized way. David wrote this paragraph to share information about an interesting pyramid in Mexico called Chichén Itzá.

> Chichén Itzá
> by David Urban
>
> A place called Chichén Itzá has one of the biggest pyramids in Mexico. The name of this pyramid means "Mouth of the Wells of Itzá." It is over a thousand years old and was built by the Itzá group of the Mayan Indians. This pyramid has many stairways. They lead to rooms with walls covered with colored paintings and stone carvings. Near the pyramid is the Great Ball Court, where games were played. There is also an observatory where the people studied the stars and planets. Today many people visit this pyramid and other pyramids in Mexico.

Talk About the Model

★ What does this paragraph inform the reader about?

★ How does the writer introduce the subject?

★ Which details give you a clear picture of the subject?

Make a Plan

What topic will you inform readers about? As you choose a topic, don't take on more than you can explain in one paragraph. If your topic seems too big, narrow it. David chose to write about one pyramid.

Once you narrow your topic, think about these questions as you plan what you will write.

• What will my audience want to know about my topic?

• What facts and examples should I include?

Write It Down

1. Begin with a sentence that lets readers know what they will be learning about.

2. In the middle, give examples and details that tell about your subject.

3. Organize your ideas. Be clear and make your writing easy to follow.

Conferencing

Read your informative paragraph to a small group. Do your classmates understand what you have explained? Is there information you should add?

Look It Over

Reread your paragraph. Does each sentence give more information about your main idea? Do you use complete sentences?

Tech Tip

If you are using a computer, it's easy to insert more examples and details if needed.

Portfolio

Since you might want to publish your paragraph, keep it with the notes you've made.

Writing a Friendly Letter and Envelope

Letters from friends, a family member, or a pen pal are very special. A **friendly letter** is a written message to a friend or relative, sharing your thoughts, your feelings, and what's happening in your life.

Usually it's not polite to read other people's letters. In this case, it's OK to snoop a bit. Here is a letter from one friend to another. It appeared in a book called *Amber Brown Goes Fourth* by Paula Danziger.

Dear Justin,

Thanks for writing to me. I wish you were here. (You probably wouldn't like being here because I'm in detention . . . which I got because I kind of lost my head in Elementary Extension.)

Oh, I added the used gum you mailed me to our gum ball. It was a good idea to put a wet paper towel around it and put it in a baggy (it did leak a little). I'll keep adding to the ball, too. I just wish that you could add the gum yourself.

I also wish your handwriting was better. I wish to ask you a few questions about your new school's lunch menus (since it's so hard to read your handwriting): Do they serve worm rolls? Or warm rolls? Did you really have to eat pimpled feets? Or was it pickled beets? (Either one sounds gross!) Do the kids at your school really call the cafeteria hamburger that? Wow!

Oh, you know what? I'm becoming friends with Brandi Colwin. She's really nice . . . You'd like her.

I hope that you have a new friend, too. (Just don't like him or her more than you like me.)

Your friend,

Amber

P.S. Don't eat too many worm rolls.

Talk About the Model

As a Reader

★ How do you know that this is not the first letter Amber and Justin have written to one another?

★ What can you tell about the person who will get the letter?

★ Why does the writer ask her friend so many questions?

As a Writer

★ How many subjects does the writer cover in her letter?

★ What details does the writer include to make her letter enjoyable and interesting for her reader?

★ How does the writer make the closing of her letter special?

Greeting

The writer tells news and asks questions in the body of the letter.

Sender's name and address

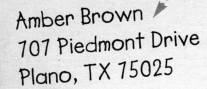

Amber Brown
707 Piedmont Drive
Plano, TX 75025

Justin Daniels
148 Bates Road
Columbus, OH 43216

Closing

Signature

The writer adds a thought.

Receiver's name and address

More About a Friendly Letter

A friendly letter has five main parts: the **heading, greeting, body, closing,** and **signature.**

Dear Pen Pal,

Heading

The heading goes in the top right-hand corner of a letter. It includes your address and the date. In the model, Amber did not write a heading in her letter to Justin. This is what a heading looks like.

> 707 Piedmont Drive
> Plano, Texas 75025
> August 19, 1999

Greeting

The greeting of a letter usually begins with *Dear* and is followed by the name of the person who will receive the letter. Add a comma after the name.

Body

The body of the letter follows the greeting. The writer can share news, send messages, and ask or answer questions. Indent the first line of the paragraph. Justin might begin his letter like this.

> Dear Amber,
>   Thanks for your letter. I have loads of news to tell you. First, let me answer all of your questions.

Closing

Your buddy,

Once you have written all your messages, you write a closing. This lets your reader know that your letter is finished. Whichever closing you use, begin the first word with a capital letter and put a comma at the end.

> Your friend,   Sincerely,   Yours truly,
> Your grandson,   Love,   Your pen pal,

Signature

End your letter with your signature. Your name goes under the closing.

> Your friend,
> Justin

Make a Plan

Are you ready to write a letter? Choose a person you will write to and think about what you want to tell this person.

Choose a Person to Receive Your Letter

Write to a person you do not see every day. It might be a person who wrote to you or someone you enjoy sharing news with in a letter.

- a relative who lives far away
- a friend who moved away
- a new pen pal

Decide What You Will Write

The body of your letter has all the good stuff in it. You can write about anything and everything you want. Check out your journal. You might find something in there you want to share.

- Share news about yourself, your family, and your friends.
- Send an important message.
- Share your thoughts and ideas.
- Ask questions.

Organize Your Letter

To remember everything you want to write in your letter, try making a list. Jot down all the details you want to share. For each new topic you write about in your letter, you will begin a new paragraph.

- my birthday trip to Washington, D.C.
- thanks for the gift
- Our friend Casey got a new dog named Wolfie.
- Are you going to come for a visit?

Writer's Tip
To plan a letter, say to yourself, "I am writing a letter to ___ because I want to tell about ___."

Write It Down

Choose interesting stationery or create your own.
Remember to make your letter sound like you.
Write as if you were speaking to the person.

Include the Five Parts of a Letter

- At the top of the page, put your heading.
- Next, write your greeting.
- Now comes the best part—the body of your letter. Look back at your list to keep in mind everything you want to write.
- In the closing, say goodbye and end with your signature.

Address Your Envelope

- Write your name and return address.
- Write the name and address of the person who will receive your letter.
- Fold your letter so that it fits in the envelope.

Writer's Tip
Write your envelope neatly and legibly so that the post office will have no trouble delivering it.

Tech Tip
Send a copy of your letter by E-mail.

Conferencing

Ask a partner to check that your letter is readable and that the envelope is correctly addressed.

Look It Over

Check your letter. Have you left out something? You can add a postscript, or P.S. Is the state abbreviation and ZIP code correct in each address?

Send Your Letter

Check to be sure the envelope is addressed correctly. Don't forget the stamp. Think about including photos or drawings, too.

In the Spotlight

An **interview** happens when one person asks another person questions to get information and then writes an article about it. When was the last time you saw an interview on TV with your favorite athlete or read a magazine article about a famous musician or author? Interviews are very popular and fun to watch and read.

Meet the Writer

I interviewed my uncle, who lives next door to me. He always seems happy about going to work, so I asked him about his job.

Sheryl Palmer
Pennsylvania

An Interview

★ Identifies the person being interviewed
★ Includes questions about one or more topics
★ Gives the person's answers to these questions
★ Includes one or more paragraphs for each topic discussed
★ Includes some of the person's actual words in quotation marks

Think It Through

Your first step as an interviewer is to select a topic you want to learn more about or a person you want to know more about. Decide what questions you will ask. Then you are ready to start the interview and begin taking notes.

Brainstorming

Begin your search for a candidate to interview by deciding what you want to know. If you want to know information about a topic, think about who you could ask. If you are curious about the life or work of certain people, you may want to interview one of them.

Sheryl's List

- my uncle—working for a big company
- basketball coach—coaching kids
- Officer Paul—training to become an officer
- Mrs. Kohl—owning a pet store

List the names of people you know whom you would enjoy interviewing—a friend, a neighbor, a relative, a teacher, a business owner. Next to each name, write a topic you would ask the person about.

Select a Topic

To choose a person to interview, ask yourself questions like these.

- What am I interested in finding out?
- What will interest my readers?
- Which person can share that information with me?
- Will he or she be willing to be interviewed?

Now pick your candidate and set up a time for the interview.

Design a Plan

Sheryl chose to interview her uncle to find out about his job because her class was studying careers. She prepared questions and set up a time for the interview.

To keep in mind the purpose of her interview, Sheryl wrote her goal at the top of the paper. Then she listed her questions.

Conduct the Interview

Sheryl followed these tips.

- Ask simple questions.
- Listen carefully and take notes.
- Add questions to get more information such as *What do you mean? Why do you feel that way?* or *Can you give me an example?*

Sheryl's Questions

I will interview my uncle to learn about his career.

1. Where do you work?
2. What is your job?
3. How long have you worked there?
4. What made you take the job you have now?
5. Do you like your job? Why or why not?
6. If you had a choice, would you stay at your job or leave it?
7. If you didn't work there, what would you like to do?

Your Turn

Think about the purpose for your interview and what you want to find out. Then prepare a list of questions to ask. Conduct your interview. Listen carefully and take notes. Ask more questions if information is not clear.

Writer's Tip
To stay focused on your audience, ask about things your readers will want to know.

Conferencing

- Share your interview questions with a classmate.
- Does your partner suggest ideas you can use for interview questions?
- After the interview, share your notes.
- Does your partner think you got the information you needed?

Put It Into Words

Sheryl read the notes from her interview. She organized the information to write the first draft of an article about the interview. This is what she wrote about her uncle.

Happy on the Job
by Sheryl Palmer

The opening paragraph introduces the person and topic.

My uncle, Delvert Williams Palmer, Jr., always leaves for work wearing a smile. I was curious about his job because my class is studying careers. Uncle Delvert seemed to like his job, so I thought he would be a good person to ask about special career.

The writer gives details about her subject's job in the second paragraph.

Uncle Delvert works at VG Associates. He is a corporate tax officer. What does a corporate tax officer do? He audits corporate taxes. He said that he has worked at his job for seven years. He first choose this job because it uses his college degree in business.

The writer includes a quote.

The final paragraph tells how the subject feels about his job.

Uncle Delvert likes his job he says, "I work with professional people, and I like to do taxes. He said that if he had a choice to leave or stay with his job, he would stay. In fact he hopes to stay at his job for the next 25 years. If he did not do taxes, he would do some other type of finance job.

Think Like a Writer

As you prepare to write your article, ask yourself

★ **Subject:** Who will I write about?

★ **Audience:** Who will read the article I write?

★ **Purpose:** Why am I interviewing this person?

★ **Form:** What steps do I need to remember as I write my article?

Your Turn

Read the notes from your interview. Organize your information into paragraphs. When your main idea changes, start a new paragraph. Look at Sheryl's draft to help you plan. Each paragraph tells about a different main idea.

Drafting Checklist

- Begin your article with a paragraph that introduces the person you have interviewed.
- Write two more paragraphs to tell about your topic. Put details that tell about each main idea in a separate paragraph.
- Begin a new paragraph each time your main idea changes.
- Include the speaker's actual words in quotation marks.

Conferencing

Read your draft to a partner. What did he or she learn from it? Is your information easy to follow?

Tech Tip

If you want to remove a sentence, highlight it and use the Delete key.

Writer's Tip

Reread the notes you took during the interview. Decide what to include.

Portfolio

Keep together your interview notes. When you revise, you may need to check a detail or quote.

Take Another Look

Sheryl read her draft and decided to organize some of her details in a different way. During a conference, Sheryl's partner pointed out that she uses the same verbs too often. How do you think Sheryl improved her organization and language?

Happy on the Job
by Sheryl Palmer

My uncle, Delvert Williams Palmer, Jr., always leaves for work

wearing a smile. I was curious about his job because my class is

studying careers. Uncle Delvert seemed to like his job, so I

thought he would be a good person to ask about special career.

The writer replaces two sentences with one sentence to define a term.

Uncle Delvert works at VG Associates. He is a corporate

This means he figures out how much tax different companies owe.

tax officer. ~~What does a corporate tax officer do? He audits~~

~~corporate taxes.~~ He said that he has worked at his job for

A sentence is moved for better organization.

seven years. He first choose this job because it uses his

college degree in business.

Uncle Delvert likes his job he says, "I work with professional

The writer uses a thesaurus to replace two overused verbs.

explained

people, and I like to do taxes. He ~~said~~ that if he had a choice to

continue

leave or ~~stay~~ with his job, he would stay. In fact he hopes to

stay at his job for the next 25 years. If he did not do taxes, he

"Not everyone likes math as I do," he says. "I am a human calculator!"

Another quote is included.

would do some other type of finance job.

Revisit your article with fresh eyes. What should you change? Look back at your interview questions and answers. Did you include everything you should have? Use this checklist to help you revise.

Revising Checklist

- Do you introduce your subject in an interesting way?
- Do the details in the article match your purpose for writing?
- Is the information clear and easy to understand?
- Do the sentences in each paragraph relate to the main idea of the article?
- Are there any other details from the interview that can be added?
- Can you add any more direct quotations to make the article more interesting?

Writer's Tip
Use a different-color pen or pencil to show your changes.

Portfolio
Keep your interview notes in your portfolio. You may want to use another quote when you revise.

Conferencing

Read your article to a small group. Ask for feedback and take notes about changes that could make your article better. Use the Revising Checklist as a guide.

Become a Super Writer

There are many ways to organize information. One important tip to remember is to include only the details that match your purpose for writing. For help with organization, see page 214 in the *Writer's Handbook* section.

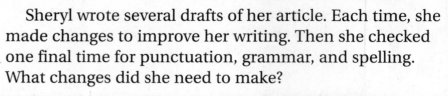
Polish Your Writing

Sheryl wrote several drafts of her article. Each time, she made changes to improve her writing. Then she checked one final time for punctuation, grammar, and spelling. What changes did she need to make?

A singular noun is changed to a plural form. •••••••••▶

Periods are added to initials. •••••••••▶

A dictionary is used to check the spelling of a problem verb form. ••••••••▶

A period and capital letter fix a run-on sentence. ••••••••▶

A quotation mark is added. ••••••••▶

Happy on the Job
by Sheryl Palmer

My uncle, Delvert Williams Palmer, Jr., always leaves for work wearing a smile. I was curious about his job because my class is studying careers. Uncle Delvert seemed to like his job, so I thought he would be a good person to ask about special career.
careers

Uncle Delvert works at V. G. Associates. He is a corporate tax officer. This means he figures out how much tax different companies owe. He first ~~choose~~ *chose* this job because it uses his college degree in business. He said that he has worked at his job for seven years.

Uncle Delvert likes his job. He says, "I work with professional people, and I like to do taxes." He explained that if he had a choice to leave or continue with his job, he would stay. In fact he hopes to stay at his job for the next 25 years. If he did not do taxes, he would do some other type of finance job. "Not everyone likes math as I do," he says. "I am a human calculator!"

To get your article ready for publishing, proofread for spelling mistakes and punctuation errors. Then look over your work for grammar mistakes. Use this Editing and Proofreading Checklist to help you.

Proofreading Marks

¶	indent first line of paragraph
≡	capitalize
∧ or ∨	add
ℯ	remove
⊙	add a period
/	make lowercase
◯	spelling mistake
∽	move
∾	transpose

Editing and Proofreading Checklist

- Have I used capital letters when writing proper nouns?

  See page 246 in the *Writer's Handbook* section.

- Did I include capital letters, commas, and quotation marks in direct quotations?

  See page 248 in the *Writer's Handbook* section.

- Is my handwriting neat and legible?

  See page 258 in the *Writer's Handbook* section.

- Did I spell all words correctly?

  See page 259 in the *Writer's Handbook* section.

Portfolio

Keep your questions, notes, and drafts to show the steps you took to do your interview and article.

Conferencing

Share your edited article with a partner. Work together to proofread again, using the checklist as a guide. Mark changes you decide to make.

Become a Super Writer

The person you interviewed told you many things. Your audience will enjoy reading your speaker's exact words. For help in writing direct quotations correctly, see pages 248 and 257 in the *Writer's Handbook* section.

Share Your Work

Once Sheryl finished editing and proofreading, it was time to share her article. Here is the final version of her article about her uncle. Sheryl made a copy of it, decorated it, and sent it to her uncle, along with a thank-you note.

Happy on the Job
by Sheryl Palmer

My uncle, Delvert Williams Palmer, Jr., always leaves for work wearing a smile. I was curious about his job because my class is studying careers. Uncle Delvert seemed to like his job, so I thought he would be a good person to ask about special careers.

Uncle Delvert works at V.G. Associates. He is a corporate tax officer. This means he figures out how much tax different companies owe. He first chose this job because it uses his college degree in business. He said that he has worked at his job for seven years.

Uncle Delvert likes his job. He says, "I work with professional people, and I like to do taxes." He explained that if he had a choice to leave or continue with his job, he would stay. In fact he hopes to stay at his job for the next 25 years. If he did not do taxes, he would do some other type of finance job. "Not everyone likes math as I do," he says. "I am a human calculator!"

It's your turn to introduce your special person or topic to an audience. Here are some ways to publish your article.

Send It Out ▶

Send a copy of your finished article to the person you interviewed.

- Make a new copy of your article. You can write it by hand or use a computer.
- Decorate the article with a colorful border or pictures.
- Write a thank-you note to the person you interviewed.
- Mail both the article and the note to the person.

◀ Talk Show

Create your own talk show to perform your article for your class.

- You pose as the person you interviewed.
- Give the original interview questions you wrote to a classmate.
- Have your classmate ask you the questions, and you can give the answers your subject did.

Human Interest Stories ▶

With other members of your class, publish an interview magazine. Include copies of everyone's interview articles. Write up a short "About the Author" blurb about yourself to include with your interview. You might want to tell why you were interested in the person you chose for the interview.

Writing a How-to Article

Have you ever wanted to make a movie, build a tree house, or walk on stilts? How would you know where to begin? What you need is a set of instructions that explains each step. A **how-to article** explains how to do or make something. It gives complete, step-by-step instructions that are clear and easy to follow.

Dawn wrote her article to explain the steps of karaoke. Since she enjoys it, she thought her classmates would be interested, too.

The beginning introduces the topic and tells why someone would want to do it.

The middle lists the materials that are needed.

Anyone for Karaoke?
by Dawn Keefe

In karaoke, YOU are the show. All eyes are on you as you sing the words to a song as the music is played. If you enjoy singing and performing, then you will find karaoke to be a great way to use your talent and have fun with a group of friends. You may even want to enter a karaoke contest.

To sing karaoke, all you need is a song, a mirror, and a cardboard tube for a microphone. First, pick a good song. It can be any kind of song like pop, rock, hip-hop, or country. It needs to be a song with words that you have on CD or cassette.

The writer explains the steps in order.

Bravo

Talk About the Model

★ What helps you picture each step as it is explained?

★ Does karaoke sound like something you might like to try? Why or why not?

★ What does the writer do to keep the instructions clear and simple?

★ Why is it important for the writer to choose a topic that she knows about and is interested in?

Play the song over and over. Sing along until you know all the words. In a real karaoke contest, the words will be on a screen so that you can read them, but it's better if you know them by heart!

Next, work on your sound. Turn the music low enough to hear yourself, but loud enough to hear the music in the background. Practice until you sing the song just right. Create your own style.

Then, think about how to act on stage. Take your microphone and stand in front of a mirror. Sing as you would in front of an audience. Do some dance moves like those that singers do when they perform.

The next time you have a get-together with friends, have some fun with karaoke. When a karaoke contest comes to town, you'll be ready!

Words like *first*, *next*, and *then* tell the order of each step.

The writer ends by telling the result of the experience.

Make a Plan

Before you write your how-to article, choose a topic and organize yourself with a plan.

Pick a Topic

Choose something you know how to do well, such as giving

- instructions that tell how to do or make something.
- an explanation of how something works.
- directions for getting to a certain place.

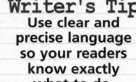

Organize Your Explanation

Imagine yourself doing each step. Make a chart like this to organize what you will write.

Writer's Tip
Use clear and precise language so your readers know exactly what to do.

How to:

Things You Need:

Steps to Follow:
1.
2.
3.

End Result:

Write It Down

As you write your article, explain your steps clearly.

- In the beginning, introduce your topic and tell why someone would want to know this.
- In the middle, name materials your reader needs.
- Write one or more paragraphs to tell your readers what to do. Use order words *first*, *next*, *then*, and *finally*.
- End with a comment or added information.

Portfolio

Save your draft. You might decide to submit it to a class newspaper or magazine.

Look It Over

Check your how-to article. Can you add details to explain more clearly? Did you include verbs that tell your reader exactly what to do?

Reporting the Facts

Do you have a younger brother or sister who is always asking *why* questions? When you have a question, where do you go for the answer—an expert, books, magazines, encyclopedias, or a Web site on the Internet?

Hunting for information about a subject is research. A **research report** is a written report that presents the information you gather from different sources in an organized way. With a topic you enjoy, research can be exciting and rewarding.

Meet the Writer

My cousins live on a farm. When I visit them, I love to watch the pigs—they're so smart! I decided to write my report about them.

Wayne
Corderro
Bowers
Florida

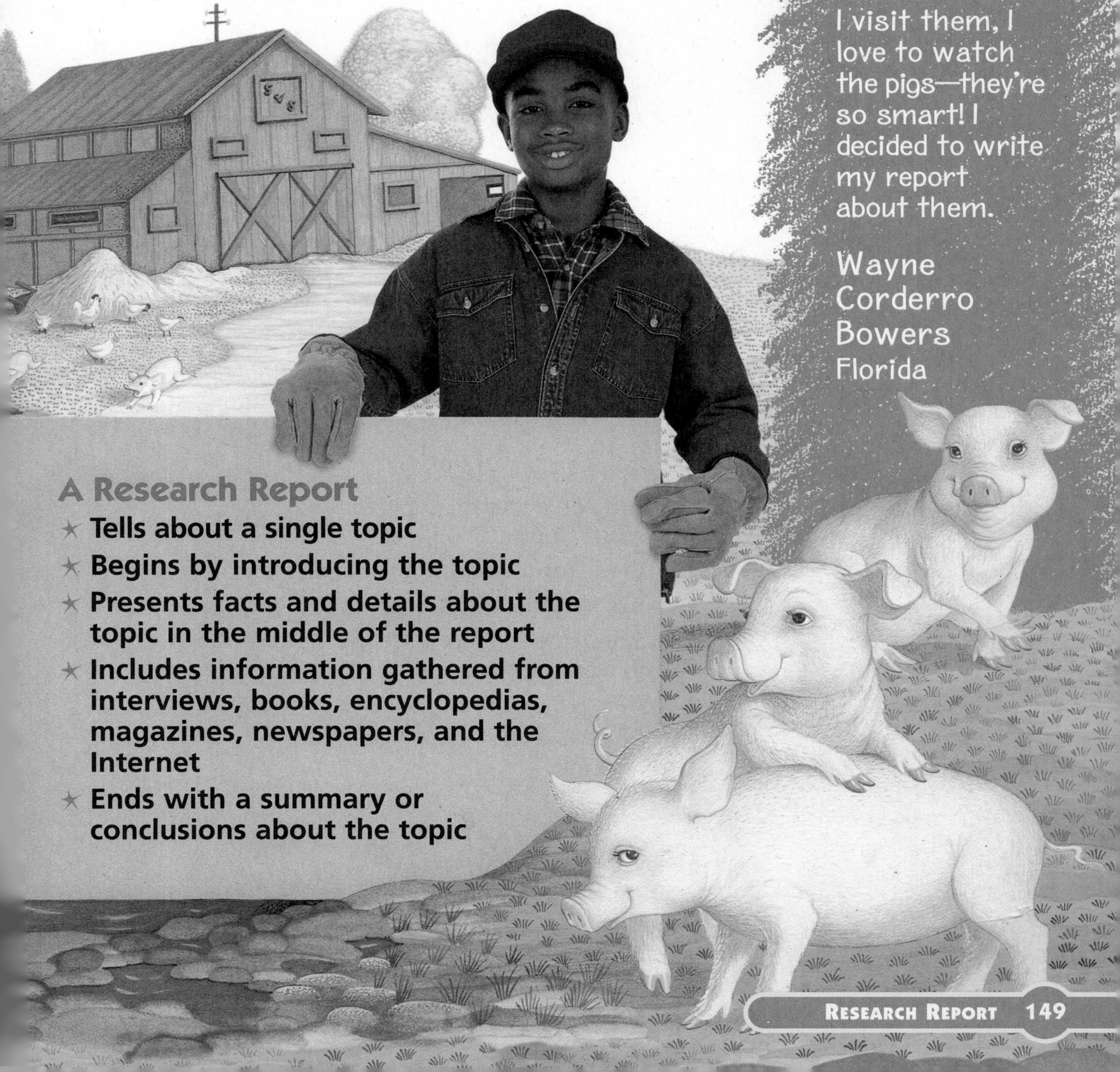

A Research Report

★ **Tells about a single topic**
★ **Begins by introducing the topic**
★ **Presents facts and details about the topic in the middle of the report**
★ **Includes information gathered from interviews, books, encyclopedias, magazines, newspapers, and the Internet**
★ **Ends with a summary or conclusions about the topic**

Think It Through

Does writing a research report sound like an awesome task? Don't worry. Getting ready to write a report is as easy as counting to five. Here's what you need to do.

1. Choose a great topic. Make it specific.
2. Make a chart to plan what you know and what you need to find out about your topic.
3. Look for information in different places. Take notes.
4. Put your notes in order. Figure out the main ideas and details you want to cover.
5. Make an outline to plan your report.

Step 1

Brainstorm and Select a Topic

What topics do you want to learn more about? What topics would interest an audience? Look in your Learning Log for ideas. Then make a cluster of your ideas.

Choose one idea for your topic. If it is too general, narrow your topic. Wayne chose the topic farm life. Look at what Wayne did to narrow his topic to pigs.

Saturn's Rings

Chickenpox

Research Topics

Giraffes

Farm Life

Decide on a specific topic for your research report.

- Brainstorm alone or with a partner.
- Record your topics in a cluster.
- Select the topic you are most interested in learning more about.
- Narrow your topic so it's specific enough to cover in one report.

Your Turn

Farm Life

Animals on a Farm

Pigs

Design a Plan

Wayne decided to write a report to inform his classmates about raising pigs on a farm. He thought about what he already knows about pigs and what he needed to find out. Then he made this chart.

What I Know	What I Need to Find Out	Where I Can Look
Pigs have curly tails, snouts, and hooves.	What are baby pigs and adult pigs called?	Ask an expert— Uncle Jake
There are different-color pigs.	Why do pigs like mud so much?	CD-ROM encyclopedia
We get food products from pigs.	What other products do we get from pigs?	Internet library—books and magazines

Make a chart like Wayne's.

- List what you know about your topic.
- Write questions you want to ask.
- List sources to find your answers.
- As you begin to research, add new questions you wonder about.

Portfolio

Keep together all research-related materials. You want to make sure that nothing gets misplaced.

Look for Information

Where will you find the information you need to write about your topic? Head for the library! A librarian can help point you in the right direction by suggesting books or helping you find information.

Turn the page to find out more about resources you can use to do research.

Use a Card or Computer Catalog

A good place to search for a book is in the card or computer catalog. The **card catalog** is a collection of cards that are filed alphabetically in drawers. There are *title cards* for every book in the library. There are also *author cards* and *subject cards*. A *call number* on each card tells where to find the book on the shelves.

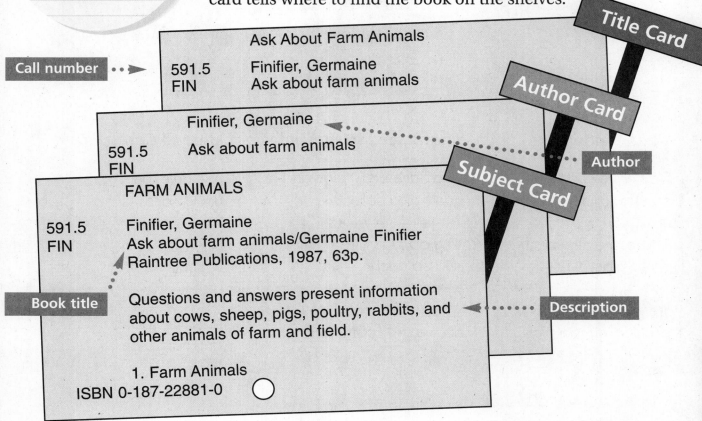

Call number

Title Card

Author Card

Subject Card

Author

Description

Ask About Farm Animals

591.5 FIN   Finifier, Germaine
Ask about farm animals

Finifier, Germaine
591.5 FIN   Ask about farm animals

FARM ANIMALS
591.5 FIN   Finifier, Germaine
Ask about farm animals/Germaine Finifier
Raintree Publications, 1987, 63p.

Questions and answers present information about cows, sheep, pigs, poultry, rabbits, and other animals of farm and field.

1. Farm Animals
ISBN 0-187-22881-0

Book title

If your library has an electronic **computer catalog**, type in a keyword. Wayne can type the keyword *pigs.*

Use Other Resources

After searching for information in books, the librarian suggested other resources for Wayne to use.

- An encyclopedia provides general information about many topics. An almanac is a book of facts. See pages 272–273 and 275 in the *Writer's Handbook* section.

- Use a computer to access information on the Internet or use an interactive CD-ROM encyclopedia.

- Magazines have articles with up-to-date information.

- An interview with an expert is a valuable source of information.

Take Notes

Once you begin to find information for your report, keep track of all the facts by taking notes.

- Use a separate note card for each question and answer.
- Write your source of information on the card.
- If you find many useful facts in one place, write a summary on the card.

Why do pigs like mud so much?
source: CD-ROM encyclopedia
    Pigs don't go in the mud to get dirty. Pigs are clean. They go in mud to cool off from the sun. Pigs don't sweat. The mud keeps bugs away, too.

Here are two of Wayne's note cards.

What products do we get from pigs?
source: interview with Uncle Jake
- pork chops, bacon, sausage, and other meats
- pigskin baseball gloves and suitcases
- paintbrushes and hairbrushes from pig bristles

Begin your research by looking for answers to each of your questions. Follow the steps that Wayne did to find information and take notes. Make use of every source of information that is available. If one source does not give enough facts, try another one.

Step 4 Organize Information

Wayne found answers to all of his questions about pigs. He looked over all the information he found and sorted his cards into these main ideas.

- what pigs look like
- how pigs act
- members of pig families

Step 5 Make an Outline

Wayne used the order of his cards to figure out what he would include in the beginning, middle, and end of his report. He made this outline to plan what he would write.

All About Pigs

I. Introduction
II. What pigs look like
   A. Body features
   B. Colors of pigs
III. How pigs act
IV. Pig families
V. Products from pigs
   A. Foods
   B. Other products
VI. Closing thoughts
   about pigs

Your Turn

Sort your note cards according to main ideas. Figure out what information you will include in the beginning, middle, and end of your report.

Make an outline to organize what you will write. Include a title, an introduction, and a closing. Include each main idea you want to write about. List details under each main idea.

Conferencing

Show your note cards and outline to a partner. Ask if the main ideas make sense and whether your details relate to the main ideas. Jot down notes to make any changes.

Put It Into Words

Here is Wayne's first draft. The second page of his draft is on the next page. Wayne begins with an introduction. How many main ideas does he cover in his report?

Discovering Pigs
by Wayne Corderro Bowers

Have you ever seen a pig? Well, I have. A pig is like no other animal. I think they are so interesting that I wanted to learn more about them.

Introduction

If you want to know a pig when you see it, you need to know what they look like. Pigs have big snouts, pointed funny ears, and curly tails. Pigs have short, thick bodies. Their skin is covered with bristles. Their feet have four toes, but they only use two.

First main idea

You may know many pigs are pink, but pigs can be all kinds of colors. That's what my uncle told me. Some are brown like chocolate. Some pigs are black and pink. Pigs can be a mix of pink white, black, and brown.

Second main idea

If you think pigs sweat, you're wrong. They need to go in the mud to cool off and keep bugs away. Pigs don't know how to talk. Pigs squeal when they are excited. They can also grunt. They are easy to train as pets. Pigs are some of the smartest animals.

Third main idea

This is the second page of Wayne's draft. After you finish reading it, compare it with his outline. Did Wayne follow his outline to write his report?

page 2

Fourth main idea

Pigs have families. A mother pig is called a sow. The father is called a bore. Babies are called piglets.

Fifth main idea

Pigs are useful. We get a lot of food from pigs that you may eat every day. Bacon comes from pigs. Ham and other meat products are also from pigs. Besides food, other things are made from pigs. Baseball gloves are made from pigskin. Suitcases are made from pigskin, too. People make paintbrushes and hairbrushes from a pig's bristles.

Closing

I think pigs are just great. They are smart and clean. They make good pets. Pigs give us food and other products we need. I hope you find pigs as interesting as I do, now that you know more about them!

Think Like a Writer

As you write a first draft of your research report, ask yourself.

★ **Subject:** What topic will I research and report on?

★ **Audience:** Who will learn from reading my report?

★ **Purpose:** Why do I want to write a report about this topic?

★ **Form:** What do I need to include in my research report?

Now it's time to write a draft of your research report. Your purpose is to give the facts and ideas about your topic as clearly as possible. Follow your outline as you write. This Drafting Checklist will also help you as you write.

Drafting Checklist

- Write an opening that introduces your topic in an interesting way.
- Begin a new paragraph for each main idea.
- Include details that tell about the main idea.
- End with a summary of the facts. Add your final thoughts about your topic.
- Give your report a title that states your topic.

Tech Tip
Print a copy of your draft to share with a partner. Mark changes you want to make on this copy.

Writer's Tip
Don't overwrite. Include only the facts that are important.

Conferencing

Read your draft to a small group of classmates. Do they understand your report? Can they give a brief summary of what you've written?

Take Another Look

Wayne took a few days off from his writing. When he read his draft again, he made additions to improve the middle paragraphs in his report. What did Wayne decide to add and why?

The writer transposes two words. •••••••••••••••➤

If you want to know a pig when you see it, you need to know what they look like. Pigs have big snouts, pointed (funny)

ears, and curly tails. Pigs have short, thick bodies. Their skin is

Descriptive details are added. •••••➤

stiff hair called
covered with bristles. Their feet have four toes, but they only
walk on two of them
use two.

The writer includes a direct quote. •••••••••••➤

You may know many pigs are pink, but pigs can be all kinds of
He's a farmer. He said,
colors. That's what my uncle told me. "Some are brown like

chocolate. Some pigs are black and pink. Pigs can be a mix of

A topic sentence is added to begin a paragraph. ••••➤

pink white, black, and brown."
Pigs are different from other animals.
If you think pigs sweat, you're wrong. They need to go in the

A sentence that is off the topic is taken out. ••••➤

mud to cool off and keep bugs away. Pigs don't know how to
talk. Pigs squeal when they are excited. They can also grunt. They

A sentence is moved to improve organization. •••➤

are easy to train as pets. (Pigs are some of the smartest animals.)
Did you know pigs have families? Well, they do.
Pigs have families. A mother pig is called a sow. The father is

A question and answer are added for sentence variety.

called a bore. Babies are called piglets.

Now it's time to revise your research report. Do you like how it turned out? What are your favorite parts? How could you make it even better? Use this Revising Checklist to help you improve your draft.

Revising Marks

≡   capitalize

∧   add

   remove

⊙   add a period

/   make lowercase

◯   move

∿   transpose

Revising Checklist

- Does the title tell the topic of the report?
- Does the first sentence introduce the topic in an interesting way?
- Are the main ideas given in order?
- Are all the facts explained clearly?
- Can information be added to clear up a point?
- Do all the facts relate to the topic?
- Do you end the report by summing up the facts and giving some final thoughts?
- Do you include a variety of sentence types to add interest for your reader?

Tech Tip
As you work, save each draft in a new file. Label them Draft 1, Draft 2, and so on.

Conferencing

Read your research report to a classmate. Does the title name your specific topic? Have you included enough details in each paragraph to tell about the main idea? Can your partner follow the order of your paragraphs? Use the Revising Checklist as a guide.

Writer's Tip
Save all your drafts until you have finished your report.

Become a Super Writer

A combination of different types of sentences, such as questions followed by statements, makes a report interesting to read. To learn how to use a variety of sentence types, see page 219 in the *Writer's Handbook* section.

Polish Your Writing

After writing a few drafts, Wayne was satisfied with his report. It was time to check for corrections he needed to make in grammar and spelling. Can you give a reason for each correction Wayne made to the middle section?

A pronoun is replaced and a verb form is changed to make the pronoun and verb agree.

If you want to know a pig when you see it, you need to

know what ~~they look~~ ^it looks^ like. Pigs have big snouts, funny pointed

ears, and curly tails. Pigs have short, thick bodies. Their skin is

covered with stiff hair called bristles. Their feet have four toes,

but they only walk on two of them.

You may know many pigs are pink, but pigs can be all kinds of

colors. That's what my uncle told me. He's a farmer. He said, "Some

are brown like chocolate. Some pigs are black and pink. Pigs can

A comma is added in a series.

be a mix of pink, white, black, and brown."

Pigs are different from other animals. If you think pigs

sweat, you're wrong. They need to go in the mud to cool off

and keep bugs away. Pigs squeal when they are excited. They

A prepositional phrase is added.

can also grunt. Pigs are some of the smartest animals ^in nature^ .

They are easy to train as pets.

The spelling of a homonym is corrected.

Did you know pigs have families? Well, they do. A mother pig

is called a sow. The father is called a (bore.) ^boar^ Babies are called

piglets.

Read your report as if you've never seen it before. Look for spelling, punctuation, and grammar mistakes. Use this Editing and Proofreading Checklist to help you polish your work.

Proofreading Marks

¶	indent first line of paragraph
≡	capitalize
∧ or ∨	add
✐	remove
⊙	add a period
/	make lowercase
◯	spelling mistake
∽	move
∾	transpose

Editing and Proofreading Checklist

- Did I use capital letters when I wrote the title of my report?

  *See page 250 in the **Writer's Handbook** section.*

- Did I spell all the words (especially homonyms) correctly?

  *See pages 259–267 in the **Writer's Handbook** section.*

- Does each prepositional phrase show how a noun or pronoun is related to another word in the sentence?

  *See page 245 in the **Writer's Handbook** section.*

- Did I punctuate direct quotations correctly?

  *See page 257 in the **Writer's Handbook** section.*

Conferencing

Show your corrections to a classmate. Does your partner see other changes you need to make? Use proofreading marks to show what you will do.

Tech Tip
Use the arrow keys to scroll to different parts of your report.

Portfolio
Store your final draft in your portfolio with all your prewriting papers until you are ready to publish.

★ Become a Super Writer

Details can often be added by using prepositional phrases. To learn how and to discover a choice of prepositions you can use, see page 245 in the *Writer's Handbook* section.

Share Your Work

Here is Wayne's completed research report. Wayne decided to publish his report by giving a slide presentation to the class. He took photographs of the pigs on his uncle's farm to present with his report.

Discovering Pigs
by Wayne Corderro Bowers

Have you ever seen a pig? Well, I have. A pig is like no other animal. I think they are so interesting that I wanted to learn more about them.

If you want to know a pig when you see it, you need to know what it looks like. Pigs have big snouts, funny pointed ears, and curly tails. Pigs have short, thick bodies. Their skin is covered with stiff hair called bristles. Their feet have four toes, but they only walk on two of them.

You may know many pigs are pink, but pigs can be all kinds of colors. That's what my uncle told me. He's a farmer. He said, "Some are brown like chocolate. Some pigs are black and pink. Pigs can be a mix of pink, white, black, and brown."

Pigs are different from other animals. If you think pigs sweat, you're wrong. They need to go in the mud to cool off and keep bugs away. Pigs squeal when they are excited. They can also grunt. Pigs are some of the smartest animals in nature. They are easy to train as pets.

Did you know pigs have families? Well, they do. A mother pig is called a sow. The father is called a boar. Babies are called piglets.

Pigs are useful. We get a lot of food from pigs that you may eat every day. Bacon comes from pigs. Ham and other meat products are also from pigs. Besides food, other things are made from pigs. Baseball gloves are made from pigskin. Suitcases are made from pigskin, too. People make paintbrushes and hairbrushes from a pig's bristles.

I think pigs are just great. They are smart and clean. They make good pets. Pigs give us food and other products we need. I hope you find pigs as interesting as I do, now that you know more about them!

Now it's time for all your hard work to pay off! Share your finished research report with an audience. Here are some ways you can publish your report for classmates, friends, and family to enjoy.

Slide Show ▶

If you are able to take photographs of the subject of your research report, you might consider doing a slide presentation.

- Take photographs. Have them developed as slides.
- Arrange your slides in order in your school's slide projector.
- Set up a screen.
- Present your research report while showing slides to your class.

◀ Presentation to the Class

Pick a day to present your work to classmates as an oral report. Share the interesting facts you learned. Make a display of pictures, charts, or graphs that present the information you are sharing. After all that research, you are an expert!

Sing a Song of Research ▶

Take the information from your report and turn it into a song or rap that you can perform for an audience. As you sing, ask a partner to use sign language to sign the words so all your classmates can enjoy and learn from your song.

Writing a Problem-Solution Essay

Meet the Writer

Kathleen M. Kowalski wrote this article for the magazine *Girls' Life*. Her writing style makes it easy and enjoyable to read about a problem many of you face and to discover ways to find a solution.

When you have a problem, what do you do? You figure out the best way to solve it, right? A **problem-solution essay** describes a problem the reader might come across. Then it explains how to solve the problem in easy-to-follow steps.

This problem-solution essay describes a common problem you may have faced at some time or other. Luckily the writer, Kathleen Kowalski, has some great ideas about what you can do to solve it.

The problem is identified in the opening.

Steps to solving the problem are clearly explained in each paragraph.

Facts and details are provided.

Hey, It Doesn't Work

by Kathleen M. Kowalski

You couldn't wait to spin Dishwalla on your new CD player, but it only groans when you hit "play." The soles of your new shoes are practically falling off the first time you wear them. Smart consumers know how to trade in faulty items—and get their cash back.

New products often come with boring paperwork. Whatever you do, don't throw it away! It tells you how long the company guarantees the product and what to do if there's a defect. Follow instructions carefully. That way, you'll also be sure problems aren't your fault.

If a problem does arise, act quickly. Put the purchase into its original packaging, grab the receipt, and head to the store. Most will give a refund or an exchange, if you act promptly. When a salesman says, "You bought it, it's yours," don't freak. Ask calmly to see the manager. If the manager refuses to help, contact company headquarters or the manufacturer of the product. If the warranty papers tell you to ship the product back, pack it carefully and follow directions.

Talk About the Model

As a Reader

★ How does the writer tie the article to your experience?

★ Which solution do you think you would try?

As a Writer

★ Why is it important to catch your audience's attention at the beginning of an article?

★ What does the writer do to help you understand what you should do to solve a problem like this?

★ How does the writer entertain you as well as inform you?

Still bummed? Put it in writing. Keep the tone polite as you state your name, address, phone number, name and model number of the product; where and when it was bought; what you want (refund, replacement, or repair). State a date by which you want a response, and keep a copy of the letter.

Whether you're buying a CD player, backpack, or hair dryer, you're entitled to products that work. So, make your buying decisions wisely. A good company knows happy customers are the best customers.

A closing idea sums up the problem and tells how to solve it.

Make a Plan

Before you write your problem-solution essay, you'll need to choose a problem. Choose a problem your readers might have themselves. Your purpose is to help them solve it.

Identify the Problem

Think about your audience. What problems do you have in common? Brainstorm a list. You may want to refer to your journal for ideas or use the following.

- problems in school
- problems in your community
- problems with friends

Read over your list. Circle the problem you want most to solve. Write two or three sentences about why you think your topic is a problem that needs attention.

Think About What Caused the Problem

Before you think about ways to solve a problem, it helps to understand what caused it.

- You may want to discuss the problem with classmates or family members to get their opinions.
- Another way is to visualize the problem. Close your eyes and picture what happens from beginning to end. Then take notes.

Solve the Problem

Now it's time to decide how to solve the problem. It's important to list the key steps in order. It's also important to add facts and details. A chart like the one below is a useful way to organize your ideas. This is what your chart might look like.

Problem	Steps to Solve the Problem
_____	1. _____
_____	2. _____
_____	3. _____

Write It Down

As you write your essay, keep in mind that you want to inform your audience about the best way to handle a problem you all share.

Identify the Problem

- Begin your essay by telling readers exactly what the problem is.
- Be sure to include many details to get your readers involved.
- Explain why you think it is a problem.

Writer's Tip
Renumber your steps if you add new ones.

Tech Tip
Don't always use bullets. Dress up your essay. Look to see what other characters are in your symbols font.

Portfolio
Save your planning chart. Use it as an example if you write another essay.

Present Your Solution

Give your opinion of the best way to solve the problem. Keep in mind that the solution should be the best choice for others as well as for you. Follow your chart to include all the steps you would follow to take action. Add examples to help your readers understand the steps.

Conferencing

Ask a classmate to read your problem-solution essay. Is the problem clearly identified? Do you offer a solution? Does your partner agree with your solution?

Look It Over

Read your essay. Do you like what you've written? Will your readers know what to do if they ever have this problem? Revise sentences to make ideas clearer. Use an exclamation mark at the end of sentences that express strong feeling.

Writer's Tip
Stay focused on the solution. Don't get sidetracked with other concerns as you write.

Share Your Work

If you want to share your solution to a common problem, the following are some ways you can publish your essay for classmates, friends, and family.

E-mail

Send an E-mail or write a letter to a friend or family member, describing the problem. Leave out your solution and invite the other person to give a solution. When you get a reply, compare your solution with the one you received.

Tech Tip
If you want to list details, you can use bullets or look to see what other characters are in your symbols font.

Problem–Solution Roundtable

Read your problem-solution essay to a group. Pause after presenting your problem to ask your audience what they would do to solve the problem. Then finish reading your essay to share your solution.

IN MY OPINION

Writing to Persuade

Writing a Persuasive Paragraph

"I think my idea is best." We all have opinions, but how do you persuade others to see things your way? One way is to write a **persuasive paragraph** that includes reasons and examples to convince readers to agree with your opinion. In "Student Crossing Guards," Luz Morales explains why she prefers students over adults as crossing guards.

Meet the Writer

I walk to school every day. It's a nice walk . . . except for one small part. That's what I wrote about.

Luz Morales
California

Student Crossing Guards
by Luz Morales

Instead of grown-up crossing guards, I think we should have student crossing guards. We always had student guards until this school year. The student guards were nice, and they kept us safe. Then, for no reason, someone thought kids couldn't do the job. My new crossing guard is a man. He makes kids wait on the corner, even when the light says WALK. If you put one toe over the curb, he yells. I know all grown-up guards are not like this, but the student crossing guards were better. They were nice to kids because they are kids, too. Don't you agree that they should be brought back?

Talk About the Model

★ Why does the writer want to convince you that she is right?

★ What are her reasons for thinking this way?

★ Do you agree with her reasons? Why or why not?

Make a Plan

Choose a topic you care about. Think about why you believe what you do. Then make a chart to plan your writing. Write your opinion. List three reasons for your opinion and one example to back up each reason.

Opinion:	
Reasons	Examples
1.	1.
2.	2.
3.	3.

Write It Down

- State your opinion in your first sentence.
- Give three or more reasons for your opinion. Save your strongest reason for last.
- Back up your reasons with examples that will help readers understand your thinking.
- At the end, sum up your opinion in a sentence. Ask readers to agree with you or suggest that they do something about the issue.

Conferencing

Read your paragraph to a small group. Which reasons do your partners think are best? Has your paragraph changed anyone's mind?

Look It Over

Read your paragraph again. Did you give readers good reasons and examples to agree with you? How can you be more convincing?

Tech Tip

Use the Insert key to add an example or two for each reason.

Portfolio

File your paragraph. Return to it later to add reasons or examples if you choose to publish.

Writing a Brochure

How many times a day do you see a slogan or an advertisement that tries to persuade you to do something? A **brochure** is a booklet that uses information and pictures to convince the reader to do or join something.

The team of writers who put together this brochure use information, exciting captions, and great photos to persuade both children and adults.

Meet the Writers

This brochure comes from Space Camp, a program that gets students involved in learning firsthand about space and space travel. The team of writers who created this brochure want to convince kids to sign up.

The title tells the focus of the brochure.

space ca

BASIC TRAINING: During your five-day stay, you'll learn about the academics, emotions, and physical requirements it takes to be an astronaut. But at SPACE CAMP®, you don't just hear about what an astronaut does,

you'll do what an astronaut does! You'll get strapped into the 5 Degrees of Freedom simulator to train for an extravehicular activity (a space walk to most people). Experience what it takes to move around on the moon in the 1/6th Gravity Trainer.

Convincing reasons and examples are given.

Talk About the Model

As a Reader

★ What is the first thing that catches your attention?

★ Why would you want to go to this camp?

★ What is one convincing reason given for signing up?

As a Writer

★ How does the writing team present information?

★ How do the writers convince readers to go to the camp?

★ What do the writers use to create excitement?

OPEN
YEAR-
ROUND!

MAKE YOUR RESERVATION TODAY!
1-800-63 SPACE
See our Credit Payment Plan option on page 17.

Try your hand at controlling the Manned Maneuvering Unit. . .the backpack that allows astronauts to work untethered from the shuttle. Then spin like crazy in the Multi-Axis Trainer to feel what it's like to tumble in a spacecraft. **WHERE DO YOU GO?** You can attend SPACE CAMP at one of three great locations: In **Huntsville, Alabama,** you'll stay at the U.S. Space & Rocket Center, the world's largest space museum and home of the NASA Marshall Space Flight Center's official Visitor Center. You'll see the first rocket to put an American into space, along with the massive Saturn V, the rocket that took Americans to the moon. You'll journey to Jupiter on a deep space adventure, take a Mission to Mars, and you'll get to feel 4 G's of lift off force and the sensation of weightlessness on the SPACE SHOT™ simulator.

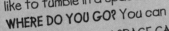

U.S. Space Camp Launch Pad

The writers provide information in words and pictures.

Vivid words create excitement.

Make a Plan

Choose a topic for a brochure. Make a chart to plan reasons why others should join or do something.

Choose a Topic

- Brainstorm names of things your readers can join, such as a club for kids, a special class, or a team.
- Brainstorm things your readers can do, such as go to a camp or visit a tourist attraction.
- Choose one idea for your brochure.

Make a Planning Chart

Make a chart to plan your brochure. List reasons and examples why your readers should join or do something.

Topic: {State what readers should join or do.}	
Reason 1: Examples:	Reason 2: Examples:

Write It Down

Create a brochure that will get readers excited.

- Give your brochure an inviting title.
- Introduce your topic in the opening paragraph.
- Present three or four convincing reasons. Give examples to back up your reasons.
- Add pictures or photos with captions.

Writer's Tip
Use colored pencils or pens to highlight key words or ideas.

Conferencing

Discuss your brochure with a group of classmates. Does it convince your partners? Jot down ideas for improvements that are suggested.

Portfolio

Save your brochure in your portfolio. You might want to send it to a friend!

Look It Over

Read your brochure again. Is it colorful and inviting? What can you add to convince your readers to join or do something? Try including adjectives or adverbs to create excitement.

Read All About It!

When you go to the library and look at all the rows of books, how do you choose which book to read? One thing that can always help you choose a good book is a book review. A **book review** tells the main ideas of a book and gives the reviewer's opinion of it. The purpose of the review is to convince others to read the book as well.

A Book Review

★ **Includes the title of the book and its author**
★ **Summarizes the story or the content of the book**
★ **Gives reasons for reading the book, with examples to support each reason**
★ **Tells what the writer liked or didn't like about the book, and why**
★ **Recommends the book to a particular group of readers**

Meet the Writer

When I read this book, I cared so much about the main character that I cried. I want to tell you why you should read this book, too.

Danielle Harrison
Iowa

Think It Through

You've probably read many books that you really like and want to persuade classmates to read as well. The first step in writing a book review is to choose the right book.

Brainstorming

Meet in small groups to talk about what you look for when choosing a book to read. Discuss books you have read recently and tell why you would read them again or lend them to a friend.

Read Me!

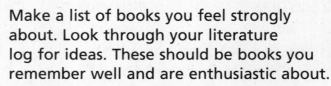

Make a list of books you feel strongly about. Look through your literature log for ideas. These should be books you remember well and are enthusiastic about.

- Which books stand out in your mind?
- Which ones were unusual in some way?
- Which books would you convince friends and classmates to read?

Danielle's List

A Picture of Freedom: The Diary of Clotee, a Slave Girl

Dear Mr. Henshaw

Wanted . . . Mud Blossom

Muggie Maggie

Pick Me!

Select a Topic

Look over the books you listed. Choose the book you liked best to write your review about. These questions can help you make your choice.

- Which book would you read again?
- Which book would you choose first to lend to a friend?
- Which book is good enough to convince others to read?

Design a Plan

Before you start your review, you will need a plan for your writing. Danielle chose the book *A Picture of Freedom: The Diary of Clotee, a Slave Girl*. She planned what she would write by making a diagram. These are the details Danielle included.

Review Me!

Title:	A Picture of Freedom: The Diary of Clotee, a Slave Girl
Author:	Patricia McKissack

My opinion: This is a fantastic book about an important time in history.

Reasons to read:	Examples:
1. To learn about American history.	People owned slaves. Slaves escaped through the Underground Railroad.
2. To learn about life as a slave.	Slaves could not go to school. Slaves had to keep their owners happy.

I'm Better!

Your Turn

Use Danielle's diagram to plan your own book review. Include strong opinions.

- State your opinion about the book you chose.
- List two or more convincing reasons why others should read the book.
- Give examples to back up each reason.

Conferencing

Share the book and your planning diagram with a classmate. Talk about why you have strong feelings about the book. Does your partner think this is a good choice?

Portfolio

Keep your notes in your portfolio. They'll be useful when you write your book review.

Put It Into Words

Here is Danielle's first draft. She kept the book nearby as she wrote so she could find details easily. How does Danielle use her prewriting diagram to write her first draft?

The writer states the book title and her opinion of the book.

A summary describes the characters, setting, and events.

Two reasons for reading the book are given, with examples.

The writer recommends the book to others.

The Diary of a Brave Person
by Danielle Harrison

A Picture of Freedom: The Diary of Clotee, a Slave Girl is a fantastic book about a twelve-year-old slave girl. The story takes place at Belmont Plantation in Virginia. Clotee lives with her aunt and uncle. She works in the kitchen of the plantation house. After Clotee secretly learns to read and write she keeps a diary.

If you like history, I recommend that you read this book. You will learn how many slaves tried to leave through the Underground Railroad. Some stayed behind as conductors to help plan these escapes.

If you read this book, you will learn what life is like for a slave. Imagine not being able to go to school. Imagine being owned by someone.

Clotee's fight for freedom made me thankful for my own freedom. If you like stories about brave characters, you'll love this book. You'll learn a lot about the history of our country.

Think Like a Writer

As you write your first draft, ask yourself these questions.

★ **Subject:** What book am I reviewing?

★ **Audience:** Who will read my book review?

★ **Purpose:** How can I persuade readers to read this book?

★ **Form:** How can I best present information about the book?

Write a review of the book you've chosen. Be sure to include what makes the book interesting or memorable so that your audience will be convinced that they should read it, too. Follow your writing plan and this Drafting Checklist as you write.

Drafting Checklist

- Introduce the book by telling its title and the author. Include your opinion of the book here or in another part of your review.
- Give a summary of the book to tell what the book is about.
- Give your first reason why others should read the book, with examples to support your reason.
- Give a second reason for reading the book, with examples.
- Close with your opinion and suggest why others might like to read the book.

Conferencing

Have a classmate read your book review. Ask if your details convinced your partner to read the book. What questions does your partner still have?

Tech Tip
Use italics instead of underlining for the book's title.

Writer's Tip
When you summarize the book, give only the most important facts or events.

Portfolio
You may want to file all book reviews in one section of your portfolio.

Take Another Look

After Danielle wrote her first draft, she chose a few details to add. She also wanted to say more about why she liked the book. How do Danielle's revisions make her review better?

The author's name is added. ·····

The Diary of a Brave Person
by Danielle Harrison

The writer adds an exclamation to get the reader's attention. ·····

Many people owned slaves in 1859!   by Patricia McKissack

A Picture of Freedom: The Diary of Clotee, a Slave Girl is a

fantastic book about a twelve-year-old slave girl. The story

takes place at Belmont Plantation in Virginia. Clotee lives

with her aunt and uncle. She works in the kitchen of the

A detail is added about the character. ·····

plantation house. After Clotee secretly learns to read and
                    to record what life is like for the slaves at Belmont
write she keeps a diary.

If you like history, I recommend that you read this book. You

will learn how many slaves tried to leave through the

Underground Railroad. Some stayed behind as conductors to

The writer expresses an opinion. ·····

help plan these escapes.
    It is important to know about slavery.
    If you read this book, you will learn what life is like for a

A question is added for variety. ·····

slave. Imagine not being able to go to school. Imagine being
    What if you had to decide to escape to freedom or stay?
owned by someone.

A sentence is moved for better organization. ·····

Clotee's fight for freedom made me thankful for my own

freedom. If you like stories about brave characters, you'll love

this book. You'll learn a lot about the history of our country.

Read your book review again. You know how you feel about the book. Do you include enough to convince your readers to agree with your point of view? Use revising marks to keep track of the changes you want to make. The questions in this Revising Checklist will help you.

Revising Marks

≡	capitalize
∧	add
ℐ	remove
⊙	add a period
/	make lowercase
◡	move
∾	transpose

Revising Checklist

- Does the review tell readers the title and author of the book?
- Do you tell what the book is about?
- Does the review offer a strong opinion of the book so your readers will want to read the book?
- Do you include at least two good reasons with examples that tell why others should read the book?

Conferencing

Share your book review with a classmate. Ask your partner to answer each question in the Revising Checklist. How does your partner think you can improve your review?

Writer's Tip
Use language that will get your readers to agree with you.

Portfolio
Store your revised draft in your portfolio until it's time to publish.

Become a Super Writer

Beginning your review with an interesting example or incident from your book can make an impression on your readers. To learn about holding your readers' attention in the beginning or ending of your writing, see the *Writer's Handbook* section, page 217.

Polish Your Writing

Danielle checked her book review and found some grammar and spelling errors in one part of her book review. Look at the proofreading marks Danielle used. What changes did she decide to make?

The Diary of a Brave Person
by Danielle Harrison

Many people owned slaves in 1859! <u>A Picture of Freedom: The</u>

Underline a title.

<u>Diary of Clotee, a Slave Girl</u> by Patricia McKissack is a fantastic

book about a twelve-year-old slave girl. The story takes place

at Belmont Plantation in Virginia. Clotee lives with her aunt

Add a comma and conjunction to join sentences.

and
and uncle. She works in the kitchen of the plantation house.

Add a comma after an introductory group of words.

After Clotee secretly learns to read and write, she keeps a

diary to record what life is like for the slaves at Belmont.

If you like history, I recommend that you read this book. You

Use a thesaurus to replace a word.

escape
will learn how many slaves tried to leave through the

Underground Railroad. Some stayed behind as conductors to

help plan these escapes.

Change a verb tense.

It is important to know about slavery. If you read this

was
book, you will learn what life is like for a slave. Imagine not

Join two sentences to form a compound predicate.

or
being able to go to school. Imagine being owned by someone.

What if you had to decide to escape to freedom or stay?

Before you share your book review with classmates, you'll want to check for grammar and spelling errors. Use proofreading marks to show the changes you need to make. This Editing and Proofreading Checklist will help you prepare to write your final copy.

Editing and Proofreading Checklist

- Have I used capital letters and underlining to write the book title correctly?
  See pages 250 and 255 in the ***Writer's Handbook*** section.
- Have I used commas and conjunctions correctly to join short, choppy sentences?
  See pages 227 and 245 in the ***Writer's Handbook*** section.
- Can I join two short sentences by writing one sentence with a compound predicate?
  See page 225 in the ***Writer's Handbook*** section.
- Have I used a comma after an introductory group of words in a sentence?
  See page 255 in the ***Writer's Handbook*** section.

Conferencing

As you explain the changes you made to a partner, ask if there is anything you missed. Listen and make final changes before publishing.

Proofreading Marks

Mark	Meaning
¶	indent first line of paragraph
≡	capitalize
∧ or ∨	add
℘	remove
⊙	add a period
/	make lowercase
○	spelling mistake
⟲	move
∽	transpose

Tech Tip

Try using larger or fancier type for the title of your book review.

Portfolio

Save your final draft in your portfolio until you are ready to publish.

Become a Super Writer

Combine short, choppy sentences to form a compound sentence, using a comma and a conjunction. For help, see the ***Writer's Handbook*** section, pages 227 and 245.

Share Your Work

Danielle's book review is finished. She made a final copy. Now Danielle is ready to share her review with her friends. She chose to make an advertisement to publish her review.

SEE HISTORY COME ALIVE!

The Diary of a Brave Person
by Danielle Harrison

Many people owned slaves in 1859! A Picture of Freedom: The Diary of Clotee, a Slave Girl by Patricia McKissack is a fantastic book about a twelve-year-old slave girl. The story takes place at Belmont Plantation in Virginia. Clotee lives with her aunt and uncle, and she works in the kitchen of the plantation house. After Clotee secretly learns to read and write, she keeps a diary to record what life is like for the slaves at Belmont.

If you like history, I recommend that you read this book. You will learn how many slaves tried to escape through the Underground Railroad. Some stayed behind as conductors to help plan these escapes.

It is important to know about slavery. If you read this book, you will learn what life was like for a slave. Imagine not being able to go to school or imagine being owned by someone. What if you had to decide to escape to freedom or stay?

If you like stories about brave characters, you'll love this book. Clotee's fight for freedom made me thankful for my own freedom. You'll learn a lot about the history of our country.

It's time to share your review with classmates. Here are some ideas about how you can publish your book review.

A Convincing Ad ▶

Make an advertisement for your book. Get a piece of colorful poster-board. In the center, place a copy of your book review. Add an attention-grabbing title. Draw a scene or small pictures to show people, the setting, or a main event. Post your ad. Invite classmates to come to you with questions about the book.

◀ Breaking News

Pretend you are a news broadcaster. It is your job to inform the public. Practice reading your book review. Read with expression and sound convincing. Then pose as a news anchor and share the "news" of a great book with your classmates.

Q & A ▶

Organize a question-and-answer session about books in your school library. Ask your librarian for help in planning.

- Bring your book to the session.
- Know all the important information from your book review.
- Let each person tell about a book and then answer the group's questions about it.

Writing a Letter to the Editor

Do you feel strongly about an issue? One way to let people know how you feel is to write a letter to the editor. **Letters to the editor** give readers a chance to share their opinions about a topic. Each letter includes reasons and examples to back up the writer's opinion.

When a summer basketball league was about to be canceled, Griffin wrote a letter to the editor to get help.

Meet the Writer

I wrote a letter to my local newspaper and got some results! My whole basketball league was happy.

Griffin Molloy
Texas

> The sender's address is included.

1231 Travis Avenue
Sumner, TX 75289
May 2, 1999

Sara Lucas, Editor
Lone Star Gazette
4566 Curtis Turnpike
Sumner, TX 75289

> The editor's address is included.

Dear Ms. Lucas:

I am writing for my summer basketball team, the Hoopmeisters. Our season is supposed to start in two weeks. Yesterday our coach told us we won't be able to play because the town is paving all four town courts. Can the city council help us change this plan? We want to play ball this summer.

The summer league is a great chance for kids to exercise. Without courts, we won't have a place to do this. It's too late to make other plans for summer activities. The league also gives us a chance to work together as a team. We won't get the chance to compete if we have no courts.

Maybe the paving could be done in the fall, when kids will be back at school. Another idea is to pave the courts one by one. Then we could switch around and still play on the other three courts. My team and I would appreciate your help.

Yours truly,

Griffin Molloy

Talk About the Model

★ What is the problem? What solutions does the writer offer?

★ What does the writer do to try to convince his readers that he is right?

★ How is the writer's language different from what would be used in a friendly letter?

The greeting tells who receives the letter.

The writer states the problem and gives his opinion.

The writer gives reasons for his opinion along with examples.

The writer offers a solution and tells why it would work.

The letter closes and a signature is added.

Make a Plan

What will you write to the editor about? It can be anything you feel is important. Here are some ideas to get you thinking.

Choose Your Topic

- What problems are you facing in school?
- What neighborhood changes do you disagree with?
- What have you heard in the news that bothers you?

Jot down answers to these questions. Look over your answers and choose your topic for a letter.

Organize Your Letter

Once you choose a topic, organize your ideas for the letter.

- Describe the problem or situation.
- Write your opinion.
- Give reasons and examples to support your opinion and suggest solutions.

Here is the plan that Griffin made to organize his letter.

> **Problem:**
> Closing the basketball courts for paving will ruin the summer league.

> **My Opinion:**
> We should find a way to pave courts and have the league, too.

> **Reasons**
>
> 1. Basketball gives kids exercise.
>
> 2. Kids learn about teamwork.

> **Examples**
>
> 1. Without courts, we have no place to exercise.
>
> 2. Playing with a team lets us compete with others.

> **Solutions**
> 1. Pave the courts in the fall.
> 2. Pave them one by one.

Write It Down

Now it's time to speak out about something you think is important. Use a business-letter form and your plan to write your letter.

Begin With Headings

Use business-letter headings to start your letter. Look at Griffin's letter on page 186. Be sure to include this in your headings.

Your Street Address
Town, State, and ZIP Code
Today's Date

Editor's Name
Name of Newspaper
Street Address
Town, State, and ZIP Code

Write Your Greeting

Look at Griffin's greeting. What punctuation did he use after it? Use a colon instead of a comma after the greeting in a business letter.

If you know the person's name, write
Dear Ms. Lucas:

If you do not know the person's name, write
Dear Editor:

Dear Sir:

Dear Madam:

Write the Body of Your Letter

Follow your plan to write the body of your letter. As you write, remember that you want your letter to sound convincing so that you will win over your reader to make the changes you want to happen. Use language that sounds businesslike.

Conferencing

Read your letter to a classmate. Listen to comments your partner has. Stay focused on your reasons for writing the letter.

Portfolio

Store your letter until you are ready to polish your writing and mail it.

Look It Over

Read your letter to yourself. Are the problem and your opinions stated in a clear way? Do you offer good reasons for change? What other points could be added to persuade your readers to think like you? Make changes and polish your letter before making a final copy to mail.

Share Your Writing

A letter to the editor is meant to have a public audience. After you revise and polish your letter, let others see it. Here are some ways you can share your letter.

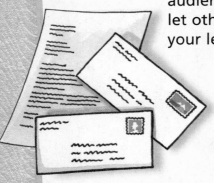

Send It Out

- Send your letter to the editor.
- Fold your letter neatly so that it fits in your envelope. Put your letter inside the envelope and seal it to be mailed.
- Address your envelope to the person who will receive the letter and include your return address. Put a stamp on the envelope.

E-Mail

E-mail a copy of your letter to a friend. Ask for your friend's opinion on the topic. Your friend might agree with you or have a different point of view. E-mail is a quick and easy way to trade ideas about an important topic!

Writer's Tip
Your letter represents you. If you write your letter by hand, be sure to write neatly.

Tech Tip
A typed letter printed on nice stationery is a good idea for a business letter.

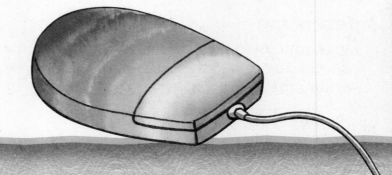

Lend Me Your Ears

Police officers give speeches about seat-belt safety. Sales people give speeches about a product they want to sell. A **speech** is a prepared talk given to an audience. The purpose of the speech might be to give information about a topic or to get listeners to agree with the speaker's point of view.

Meet the Writer

Hard work and no play is not good for a family. Families need time for fun, so I wrote a speech to tell why it's important to take a break together.

Tommy Osceola
Florida

A Speech

★ Has an interesting opening to get the attention of the audience
★ States the most important point at the beginning
★ Offers the speaker's opinions and ideas
★ Includes facts to back up each opinion
★ Repeats the most important point at the end

Think It Through

If you want your speech to persuade your audience to agree with you, keep them in mind while you plan what to say.

Brainstorm and Select a Topic

To brainstorm a topic, Tommy made a list of issues that he is interested in and knows something about. Tommy chose the importance of family vacations as his topic.

Tommy's List
1. year-round school
2. soccer teams for boys and girls
3. lanes for bikes and in-line skaters
4. the importance of family vacations

Design a Plan

Tommy made a diagram to plan his speech. He stated his opinion and included three reasons to support his opinion.

Opinion: Family vacations are necessary.

Reason 1	Reason 2	Reason 3
Families don't spend enough time together.	Families need time to relax.	Vacations can be a learning experience.

Your Turn

Make a list of topics that are important to you and others. Check your journal for ideas. Select the topic you feel strongly about. Then make a plan to state your opinion and list supporting reasons.

Conferencing

Share your diagram with a classmate. What does your partner think of your opinion as a topic? Does your partner have other reasons you should consider? Take notes as you discuss these things.

Collect and Organize Information

Here are some places to get information.

- Interview people or observe people and events.
- Read books, magazines, newspapers, and brochures.
- Visit Web sites on the Internet.
- Watch videos and TV programs.

Portfolio

Keep all your notes and outline together so you have them when you write your draft.

Make an Outline

Tommy interviewed people and visited Web sites to collect facts that would support the reasons for his opinion. He made this outline to organize his ideas.

Time-out for Family

I. Introduction

II. Families don't spend enough time together.
   A. Parents' schedules are hectic.
   B. Kids have their own weekend activities.

III. Families need time to relax.
   A. Parents work long hours.
   B. Kids have school and homework.

IV. Vacations can be a learning experience.
   A. Families can try something new.
   B. Families can travel to new places.

V. Closing

Writer's Tip

Carry a notebook to record details as you collect information.

Your Turn

Collect information that includes facts to support each reason for your opinion. Make an outline to show your opinion, reasons, and supporting facts. Include an introduction and closing.

Conferencing

Share your outline with classmates. Do you list enough reasons and facts to persuade an audience?

Put It Into Words

Here is Tommy's first draft. What reasons does the writer give to support his opinion? Do his facts persuade you to think the same way he does?

Time-out for Family
by Tommy Osceola

Introduction ······▶ I am here today to tell you why it's necessary to take a

Most important idea ···▶ family vacation. Taking a vacation together should be the most

important thing you do.

····▶ Families don't spend enough time together. Family members

First reason with facts often are not together at the same time. On weekends, kids

have activitys of their own. A vacation could be a time to do

····▶ something everyone enjoys.

····▶ Families need time out from work to relax. Parents work long

Second reason with facts hours. Kids have school during the week and homework to do at

····▶ night. A planned vacation would guarantee time together.

····▶ Vacations can be a good experience for everyone.

Third reason with facts Parents and kids gets a chance to try something new like

traveling by train camping in a national park, or exploring a

····▶ cave. A vacation can take a family to a new city or country.

Isn't it time to plan your vacation? Take my advice. Time with

Most important idea is repeated. ····▶ your family can be real relaxing and educational.

Think Like a Writer

As you write the first draft of your speech, keep these questions in mind.

★ **Subject:** What issue do I feel strongly about?

★ **Audience:** Who needs to know about my opinions?

★ **Purpose:** Why am I writing this speech?

★ **Form:** What are the characteristics of a good speech?

Tech Tip
Double-space your draft and print it. It is easier to make changes on paper.

Your Turn

You have chosen a topic for your speech, collected facts, and made an outline. Now it's time to write your speech.

Stick to your plan as you write. The most important thing is to get your ideas on paper. You can always go back and make changes later. Use the following checklist as a guide.

Writer's Tip
Leave room in the margins. Later, you'll put in reminders such as "Look up at the audience."

Drafting Checklist

- Start with an interesting introduction.
- State your most important idea first.
- Follow your outline to include each reason.
- Back up each reason with facts.
- End your speech by repeating your most important idea.
- Write a good title for your speech.

Portfolio
Keep your draft and outline with any conferencing notes you took. You will need them when you revise.

Conferencing

Read your speech to a classmate. Is your message clear? Do you use facts to support your point of view? Can you add imperative sentences to spice up your speech?

Take Another Look

After Tommy shared his speech with a partner, he felt that he could add details to make some parts sound more convincing. Look at Tommy's changes. How do you think they improve his speech?

The writer gets the audience's attention. .....▶

The writer uses an analogy to make a comparison that everyone understands. .....▶

The writer's words convince the audience that they agree with him. .....▶

An exclamation makes a point. .....▶

A more vivid word is used. .....▶

Time-out for Family

by Tommy Osceola

No one here needs a vacation! Am I right? Wrong!
I am here today to tell you why it's necessary to take a

family vacation. Taking a vacation together should be ~~the most~~
as important as eating a good breakfast or getting daily exercise.
~~important thing you do.~~

Families don't spend enough time together. Family members

often are not together at the same time. On weekends, kids

have activitys of their own. A vacation could be a time to do

something everyone enjoys.
I think you would agree that
Families need time out from work to relax. Parents work long

hours. Kids have school during the week and homework to do at
That's so important!
night. A planned vacation would guarantee time together.
learning
Vacations can be a ~~good~~ experience for everyone.

Parents and kids gets a chance to try something new like

traveling by train camping in a national park, or exploring a

cave. A vacation can take a family to a new city or country.

Isn't it time to plan your vacation? Take my advice. Time with

your family can be real relaxing and educational.

How can you improve your speech to make your audience agree with your opinion? Can you say something in another way to make your speech more exciting?

This is the time to mark changes on your draft. Use revising marks to add or change words and cross out parts you no longer need. Use the Revising Checklist to help you decide what to change.

Revising Checklist

- Did I get my audience's attention?
- Do I state each reason and fact clearly?
- Can I include an analogy to get a point across?
- Can I add language that will help me persuade my audience to think like me?
- Do I use a variety of sentences, such as statements, questions, and exclamations, to keep my listener interested?

Conferencing

Think about your speech as you read the questions in the Revising Checklist with a partner. Talk about what you should do to make an audience more interested in what you have to say.

Become a Super Writer

A great way to keep your audience interested is to use different types of sentences. To vary the length or kind of sentence, see page 219 in the *Writer's Handbook* section.

Revising Marks

≡	capitalize
∧	add
⌒	remove
⊙	add a period
/	make lowercase
∽	move
∼	transpose

Writer's Tip
Writers use analogy and irony to make a point. See pages 207 and 211 to learn more.

Portfolio
Add each draft you write to your notes and first draft. They will remind you of the progress you have made.

Polish Your Writing

Tommy revised his speech a few times before he was satisfied. He read his speech for changes he still needed to make. Look at the proofreading marks in this portion of his draft. What did Tommy decide to add or correct?

Time-out for Family
by Tommy Osceola

No one here needs a vacation! Am I right? Wrong! I am here

today to tell you why it's necessary to take a family vacation.

Taking a vacation together should be as important as eating a

good breakfast or getting daily exercise.

Families don't spend enough time together. Family members

often are not together at the same time. On weekends, kids

activities

have ~~activitys~~ of their own. A vacation could be a time to do

something everyone enjoys.

I think you would agree that families need time out from

Very often,
work to relax. Parents work long hours. Kids have school

during the week and homework to do at night. A planned

vacation would guarantee time together. That's so important!

Vacations can be a learning experience for everyone.

get
Parents and kids ~~gets~~ a chance to try something new like

traveling by train, camping in a national park, or exploring a

cave. A vacation can take a family to a new city or country.

Isn't it time to plan your vacation? Take my advice. Time

very
with your family can be real relaxing and educational.

The writer corrects the spelling of a word by changing *y* to *i* and adding *es*.

An adverb is added to tell "how often."

A verb is changed to agree with a compound subject.

A comma is added in a series.

The writer corrects the use of a problem word.

It's almost time to share your speech with an audience. Before you do, make it as perfect as possible. Use proofreading marks to show changes you want to make. Use this Editing and Proofreading Checklist to help you.

Proofreading Marks

⁋	indent first line of paragraph
≡	capitalize
∧ or ∨	add
✗	remove
⊙	add a period
/	make lowercase
◯	spelling mistake
∽	move
∾	transpose

Editing and Proofreading Checklist

- Did I include adverbs to tell how much, how often, when, or where?
  See pages 240–241 in the *Writer's Handbook* section.

- Did I use commas to set off words in a series or after introductory phrases and clauses?
  See pages 254–255 in the *Writer's Handbook* section.

- Did I spell words correctly, such as compound words and homonyms?
  See pages 266–267 in the *Writer's Handbook* section.

- Did I use problem words like <u>real</u> and <u>very</u> correctly?
  See page 241 in the *Writer's Handbook* section.

Tech Tip
Use a large size type when you print your speech so it will be easier to read to your audience.

Portfolio
Collect and store props, such as photos or charts, you might use to deliver your speech.

Conferencing

Invite a partner to help you double-check your speech. Explain the edits you have already made. Does your partner see any other corrections you need to make?

Become a Super Writer

One secret to great writing is to say precisely what you mean and to say it in a way that your audience will remember. Using adverbs can help you do this. For help, see pages 240–241 in the *Writer's Handbook* section.

Share Your Work

Tommy made a clean copy of his speech. He practiced his speech in front of a mirror at home. He also decided to use some props when he delivered his speech. This is the speech that Tommy gave to his classmates.

Time-out for Family
by Tommy Osceola

No one here needs a vacation! Am I right? Wrong! I am here today to tell you why it's necessary to take a family vacation. Taking a vacation together should be as important as eating a good breakfast or getting daily exercise.

Families don't spend enough time together. Family members often are not together at the same time. On weekends, kids have activities of their own. A vacation could be a time to do something everyone enjoys.

I think you would agree that families need time out from work to relax. Very often, parents work long hours. Kids have school during the week and homework to do at night. A planned vacation would guarantee time together. That's so important!

Vacations can be a learning experience for everyone. Parents and kids get a chance to try something new like traveling by train, camping in a national park, or exploring a cave. A vacation can take a family to a new city or country.

Isn't it time to plan your vacation? Take my advice. Time with your family can be very relaxing and educational.

Now it's time to give your speech the audience it deserves. Here are some ideas about how to share your speech with others.

Speak Out ▶

Stand in front of your class and deliver your speech. Here are some tips to remember.

Practice Your Speech

- Know your speech well.
- Say your speech aloud to yourself or with a tape recorder.
- Practice in front of friends or family members.

Present Your Speech

- Look at different places in the audience.
- Stand up tall. Don't lean on the podium.
- Move your hands to show key points.
- Use props, photographs, charts, or even slides.

◀ Roll Tape!

If you have a video camera you can use, have someone tape you as you present your speech. Look at the camera as often as you would look at a live audience. Show your videotaped speech to friends and family members.

Pass It On ▶

Submit a copy of your speech to your class newspaper. People outside your class may enjoy what you have to say! Make several copies of your published piece. Take a copy home to share with your family.

Writing a Poster

Posters advertise sports teams, music stars, and movies. You see posters in store windows, on billboards, and on buses. A **poster** may be art, but a poster is also a written announcement that tells people an important message.

When Max wrote his poster, he wanted everyone to know that he was running for fourth-grade class president. He also wanted his classmates to know why they should vote for him.

Meet the Writer

When I ran for class president, I had a lot of fun making posters to convince classmates to vote for me.

Max Bernardi
Wyoming

The heading gives a clear message.

Art supports the message.

Strong reasons are given.

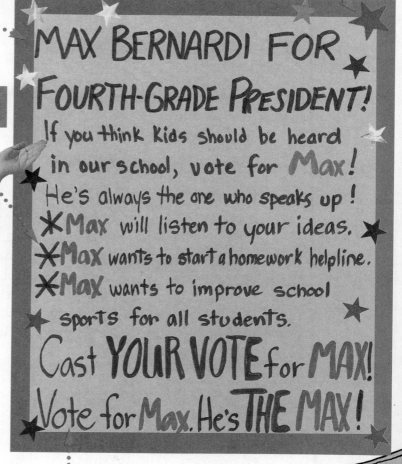

MAX BERNARDI FOR FOURTH-GRADE PRESIDENT!
If you think kids should be heard in our school, vote for Max!
He's always the one who speaks up!
* Max will listen to your ideas.
* Max wants to start a homework helpline.
* Max wants to improve school sports for all students.
Cast YOUR VOTE for MAX!
Vote for Max. He's THE MAX!

A clever slogan helps readers remember the message.

Talk About the Model

★ What is the writer's purpose? Why is a poster a good way to achieve it?

★ How does the writer share important information by using a poster?

★ Would this poster convince you to vote for Max? Why or why not?

Make a Plan

Think of a reason to create a poster. Remember that you want to convince others to think like you.

Choose a Topic

Do you have a strong opinion about a school matter? Brainstorm topics like these.

- a school election
- school lunches
- recess
- fund-raising for the school library
- school dress code
- homework

Create a Clever Slogan

Think of a short message that expresses your opinion and will get your audience's attention.

Choose Your Reasons

Think of two or more reasons that will convince others to think about your topic as you do.

Write It Down

As you create your poster, keep in mind that your purpose is to convince your readers to think like you.

Write Your Message

- Write your catchy slogan on your poster.
- Add a message that tells your opinion about the school matter you have chosen.
- Include reasons why others should agree.

Use a Great Design

- Add an eye-catching drawing or photo.
- Write with large, easy-to-read letters.

Conferencing

Show your poster to classmates. Is your message convincing? Listen to suggestions they have.

WRITER'S HANDBOOK

WRITER'S CRAFT

Alliteration is when the same beginning consonant sound is repeated in a group of words.

Alliteration creates interesting sound effects for readers. It can add humor to writing and makes words fun to read.

> The dreadful dragons dared to enter town.
>
> A dog on a long leash leaped into the yard.
>
> Many marvelous monkeys were seen munching mangoes.

Spice up stories and poems you're writing by using words that have alliteration. Begin with a key word and add other related words that begin with the same consonant sound.

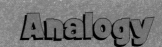

An **analogy** is a comparison of words and ideas.

Some analogies compare part to whole.

> Lead is to pencil as ink is to pen.

Some analogies compare opposites.

> Fancy is to plain as zigzag is to straight.

An analogy can also tell how two different things are alike in some way.

> Children at the toy store reminded me of bees buzzing around a garden. They flew from shelf to shelf and poked their heads into every corner of the store. What treasures would they bring home to their hives?

When you use something familiar, like bees buzzing in a garden, to make an analogy, your writing paints a clear picture for your readers. Analogies work especially well when you write to describe, to inform, or to persuade.

Remember:

In an analogy, make a comparison everyone will understand.

Character

A **character** is a person in a story. Sometimes the character is an animal that acts like a person.

Writers make characters "come alive" for readers by showing what their characters think and feel and how they interact with other characters.

In school and at home, Debbie is kind and generous and humorous. But when Debbie is on the soccer field, all she can think of is scoring a goal. To Debbie, winning the game is everything.

When you write, try to create characters who are like real people, growing and changing as the story develops.

Details

Details create a picture for the reader. Details help readers see and understand what the writer is trying to say.

Sensory Details

Sensory details describe what people see, hear, smell, taste, and feel.

Pop, pop, pop! As the kernels pop faster, the aroma of popcorn fills the room. I can't wait to grab a handful of warm kernels and taste the wonderful flavor.

Examples

Examples are facts that support a writer's opinions.

Opinion: School uniforms are a good idea.
Examples: Kids in uniforms do better in school.
               Kids look neater in uniforms.
               Uniforms save families money.

Include examples when you are writing to inform or persuade.

Remember:
The more details and examples you include, the stronger your opinion will be.

Dialogue is conversation between two or more people in a story. Writers use dialogue to let readers discover what characters are thinking and feeling.

> "I smell smoke," Diego said. "Do you think there's a fire somewhere?"

> "You bet there's a fire! And it's right next door!" Nina said. "Have you forgotten that the Carlsons invited us to a barbecue today?"

When you write dialogue, put quotation marks at the beginning and end of the speaker's exact words.

▶ **For help with quotation marks, see page 257.**

Remember:

When you write dialogue, the words should sound like real people speaking.

Exaggeration is using words to make a person or a thing seem greater than it really is. Writers use exaggeration to make a point or entertain readers.

> Our next-door neighbor is so noisy that the birds in our yard wear earplugs. He's loud even when he's asleep. People say that they can hear his snores 500 miles away!

When you write something to amuse your audience, such as a tall tale, use exaggeration to describe your subject in a larger-than-life way.

> Pecos Bill lassoes a thundercloud and squeezes every bit of water out of it so that he can enjoy a sunny day.

When you write to persuade, use exaggeration to show how important and correct your side is.

> I guarantee that if you try my recipe for Brussels sprouts, you'll want to eat them for breakfast, lunch, and dinner!

Flashback

A **flashback** interrupts a story to show what happened at an earlier time. Writers often use flashback to fill in information that readers need to know.

> Marty lay in bed feeling sorry for himself. A week ago he tried to save a cat from a tree. Just as he placed his foot on a high branch, he lost his balance and fell.
>
> "Why did I have to be such a showoff?" he wondered. He stared at the cast on his leg.

When you write a story, use flashback to show how events and actions in a character's past affect the present.

Humor

Humor is what makes people laugh. It's the ability to make readers enjoy funny things.

When you write something humorous, try to build up to the ending, just as if you were telling a joke. The best laughs usually come from amusing situations that everyone can relate to.

> I decided to make a carrot cake. I followed the recipe perfectly, I thought.
>
> Dad took a big slice of cake. After tasting it, he yelled, "Help! Get me some water!"
>
> What made the cake taste so awful? The cup of salt, of course. If only I had used sugar!

You can use humor in stories or when you write to persuade. A good laugh can help win readers to your side.

> Anyone can learn to ice-skate. Securely fasten your skates. Then position a chair in front of you to hang on to and a pillow behind you, and off you go!

An **idiom** is an everyday expression that means something different from its actual word-for-word meaning. Writers use idioms to make language more colorful and interesting.

Idiom: The cookie thief was caught red-handed.

Meaning: The cookie thief was caught taking the cookies.

Remember:
Idioms help you make your characters sound more natural.

Irony is using words to say one thing but mean the opposite. A writer can use a simple kind of irony in a character's words.

"Don't you just love beautiful, sunny days!" Maria yelled as she quickly ran to take shelter from the unexpected downpour.

Sometimes writers make irony part of the plot. For example, a writer could make a character believe that something will happen, but readers know that it will not.

"My story," said Rebecca, "will be about a very inexperienced baseball player who convinces himself that he will be named Most Valuable Player."

When Rebecca begins writing, she will show how and why the ballplayer is fooling himself.

Language

The **language** that writers use should always match their purpose and audience. Writers must think carefully about their reason for writing and who will read their work.

Formal/Informal

A person who writes a letter to the editor of a local newspaper would use **formal language**. That person is writing to an adult audience for a serious reason.

> Pets, like people, need exercise to stay healthy. I think the town should open a dog run in Franklin Park.

In a letter to a friend, the writer would use **informal language**. It matches the purpose of a friendly letter.

> We had a blast at the new dog run. You should have seen Sammi clowning around and snatching dog biscuits.

Literal/Figurative

The **literal** meaning of a word is its exact meaning. **Figurative language** uses words in an imaginative way to create word pictures. Similes and metaphors are figurative language.

Literal: Each ear has three main parts.
Figurative: Your words go in one ear and out the other.

Remember:
Use the kind of language that matches your purpose.

▶ For help with metaphors, see page 213.
▶ For help with similes, see page 220.

Metaphor

A **metaphor** is a comparison that suggests how two different things are alike in some way.

The use of a metaphor makes language interesting and colorful.

> Our friendship is a forever-blooming flower.

> Your smile is a cooling breeze on a hot summer day.

Writers use metaphors to create a feeling or to help readers picture whatever is being described. Metaphors work especially well in creative writing, such as poetry, stories, and personal narratives.

Metaphors are different from similes, which use *like* or *as* to make direct comparisons.

▶ **For help with similes, see page 220.**

> **Remember:**
> Metaphors make your writing more interesting to your readers.

Onomatopoeia

Onomatopoeia means using words that imitate the sounds they describe.

Listen to sounds in the classroom. Do you hear the creak of a chair or the *r-r-r-r-r* of the pencil sharpener? These are examples of onomatopoeia.

> Snap! Crackle! Our campfire began to roar.

> Whoosh! The kite flew high above the trees.

You can fill a story or a poem with sound by using onomatopoeia. It will let readers hear what's happening.

Order of Events and Ideas

Writers want to present their details or ideas in ways that make sense, create a clear picture, and keep readers interested.

Time

When you write to tell a story, use **time** order. Time order is the order in which events happen. Words like *first, next*, and *last* will help readers follow your story.

Space

When you write to describe, use **space** order. Organize details according to where they appear to help the reader "see" what you are describing. Use words like *in front of* and *behind*.

Importance

When you write to inform or persuade, use order of **importance**. Start with your most important idea. Then discuss your next best ideas until you end with the least important one. Use words like *most important* and *first of all* to keep readers on track.

Organization

All good writing must be organized and complete. To do this, writers make certain they have written a clear beginning, middle, and end.

Beginning

The **beginning** should catch the reader's interest. Begin a story by introducing the plot and characters. For other kinds of writing, start with a topic sentence.

Middle

The **middle** gives details about a topic or the main events of a story. Include only the details that match your purpose and put your ideas in the best order.

The **end** sums up your main ideas or tells what finally happens in a story. Don't leave readers hanging. Make sure your ending sounds like an ending.

Personification

Writers use **personification** to give human qualities to something that is not a human being.

The daffodils greeted us warmly.

The waves sang us to sleep.

Personification creates pictures in a reader's mind. These pictures help readers see, hear, or feel what happened in a fresh way.

The stubborn engine stuttered as it started. It grumbled and hesitated as the car went down the road.

Like metaphor and simile, personification is often used in stories and poems.

Remember:
I'm an example of personification because I act like a person, even though I'm not.

Plot

The **plot** is what happens in a story. Writers make sure that the series of events in a plot build on one another from beginning to end.

A plot has a **beginning** in which you set the stage for what will happen. In the **middle** you build excitement and keep readers in suspense. The story should move toward a **high point**, or climax. In the end, or **conclusion**, you show how everything turns out.

Before you begin to write, decide what the high point of your story will be. Build up to the high point and use suspense and flashback to make your characters and story events seem real and to keep your readers interested.

▶ **For help with flashback, see page 210.**

Point of View

In a story, the **point of view** identifies who the storyteller is.

First Person

In the **first-person** point of view, the storyteller is one of the characters. The writer uses words such as *I* and *me* to tell what the storyteller did and saw.

> From my room, I heard my father packing his fishing gear. Why can't I go fishing with him and my sister?

Third Person

In the **third-person** point of view, the storyteller is someone outside the story. The writer uses words such as *she, he,* and *they* to tell what happened.

> Aaron climbed the hill to the cabin. As he sat on a rock to rest, he began to wonder what his friends back home were doing.

Problem

In a story, the **problem** is the obstacle or difficulty the main character must overcome. All the events in the story center on the problem and what will happen because of it.

Sometimes the problem is between two characters or between a character and an outside force.

> The darkness made it difficult to see the trail.

Sometimes the problem is a personal struggle inside a character who is trying to make a decision.

> Carly has to choose sides in an argument among friends.

Remember:
Pick a problem that is interesting to other people.

Writers want to capture and hold their **readers' interest**. Here are some ways to do that.

Title

Grab a reader's attention by giving your work a good **title.**

> For a personal narrative: "A Dream Come True"
>
> For writing to inform: "Monster Plants"

Beginning

Your **beginning** should make your audience want to read on. Here are some different ways you can try to begin a piece of writing.

Begin with an example.

> Shipbuilders make many different kinds of ships. The newest oil tankers are so big that it takes miles at sea for them to stop.

Begin with an incident.

> Three leaves of green on a single stem meant only one thing. I had stepped into poison ivy.

> **Remember:**
> You can also begin with interesting dialogue, an action scene, a question, or a surprising fact.

Ending

A reader should feel satisfied after reading the **ending** of a story or another kind of writing. Make sure that your story ending tells what finally happened. When you write to inform or persuade, end by reminding your audience what your main ideas are and why they are important.

> If you should ever see an alligator or crocodile in the wild, know that it is not wise to get too close. They are dangerous, so watch them from a distance.

Repetition

Repetition is when a word or phrase is repeated. Writers use it in poems and other kinds of writing to add rhythm or to emphasize a certain idea.

To add rhythm: The ringing, ringing, ringing of the bells, bells, bells

For emphasis: Remember! The hammer is mine. The saw is mine. The pliers are mine. Don't lose them.

Rhyme

When writers use **rhyme**, they repeat similar sounds at the ends of words. Many poems contain end rhymes. The first two lines and the second two lines in this poem rhyme.

Have you ever seen a sheet on a riverbed?

Or a single hair from a hammer's head?

Has the foot of a mountain any toes?

And is there a pair of garden hose?

Verses that rhyme are pleasing to a reader's ear. Your poem can be silly or serious, depending on the rhymes you pick.

Rhythm

Rhythm is the pattern that sounds make. In many poems the rhythm follows a regular pattern. Stressed words or syllables come at certain fixed times.

In these lines it's easy to tell which sounds are stressed.

I often sit and wish that I

Could be a kite up in the sky.

In free verse the rhythm follows the natural flow of language.

Steady rain

falling all day long.

Drip-drop, drip-drop

covering the soccer field.

Oh, clouds!

Where have you hidden the sun?

Good **sentences** make writing clear and easy to follow. Sentences can be written in many different ways, which keep the writing interesting.

Variety

Writers spice up their writing by using a **variety** of sentence types. Read this mix of statements and questions.

> When the fire alarm rang, everyone looked up. Was this a fire drill or a real fire? We waited in single file by the door. "Don't talk," I heard the teacher say.

Length

Varying your sentence **length** can make your writing more interesting. Sometimes a short sentence that follows a few long sentences can capture the reader's attention.

> When I'm listening to the radio, I'm in another world. I enjoy floating from song to song and from station to station. Stay away.

You can also combine two shorter sentences to make one interesting longer one.

Before: I keep two frogs in this tank. I also keep a newt in this tank.

After: I keep two frogs and a newt in this tank.

Remember:

Lots of short sentences make your writing sound choppy and dull.

Beginning

Sentences don't all have to begin the same way. You can move a word or phrase to the **beginning** of a sentence.

Before: I play basketball before lunch at school.

After: At school I play basketball before lunch.

Setting

In a story the **setting** is the time and place in which the events happen. Writers often identify the setting at the very beginning of the story.

> It was 2049, the year of the Great Martian Gold Rush. Hundreds of spacecraft were on their way to the red planet. I was aboard one of them.

Choosing a unique setting that readers will want to know more about is one way that writers build interest in their stories. Your setting can be a gym, an old house, a deserted road at night, another country, an imaginary world, or any place you want. You can pick a time in the past, the present, or the future.

Simile

A **simile** is a comparison. It uses the words *like* or *as* to show that two unlike things are similar in some way. Writers use similes in poems and stories to help readers see something familiar in a new way.

> His eyes were like flying saucers.

> The cactus looked as tall as my house.

Some similes are used too much. Try to think of fresh ones.

Overused: I am as hungry as a lion.

Fresh: I am as hungry as a bear in springtime.

▶ **For help with metaphors, see page 213.**

Remember:
Use similes to
create word pictures
for your readers.

Voice is the way writers express ideas. The voice you use depends on what you're writing and why you're writing.

Lyric

When you write a description or a poem, you are probably writing with a lyric voice. A **lyric voice** lets you focus on thoughts and feelings. You pay special attention to words that paint pictures.

> Fear blinded me like a fog.
>
> My heart was a drum beating loudly.

Dramatic

Your **dramatic voice** helps you write dialogue in stories and in plays. You make your characters speak like real people.

When you write to persuade, you also use a dramatic voice. That voice wants to convince others that you're right about something.

> I have only one thing to say to you, and it is this: Vote for the person who is best for the job—me!

Narrative

Your **narrative voice** is a storyteller's voice. You are funny or serious. You build suspense. You keep your readers glued to their chairs. Sometimes you're a character in the story. Other times you tell about the characters' thoughts, feelings, and actions.

> Do you know why the wildcat has a short, stubby tail? It happened many years ago when Great Rabbit played a trick that fooled the cat. The story began one day when the wildcat went hunting for rabbits.

Remember:

Let your writing express the you behind your words.

Words

A writer chooses **words** that will make the writing clear and interesting. As you write, decide whether you need to use a more colorful or exact action word or describing word.

Precise Words

Precise words are words that get across exactly what you mean. Specific nouns and adjectives won't leave your readers guessing about what you mean.

Before: Kids here need a decent place to hang out.
After: Neighborhood kids need a youth center.

Before: Add some flour to the mixture.
After: Add one level cup of flour to the mixture.

Before: Free puppies for you!
After: Playful golden retriever puppies free to loving families!

Vivid Words

When you use **vivid words** in your writing, you create colorful images that help a reader see the scene you've described.

Before: Bettina skated across the ice rink.
After: Bettina glided gracefully across the ice rink.

Before: Hank slid on the ice and fell.
After: Hank's feet flew out from under him as he hit the patch of ice.

Before: A lot of snow filled our yard.
After: A cool thick blanket of glistening white snow covered our yard.

A thesaurus is a helpful tool when you are searching for just the right words.
▶ **For help in using a thesaurus, see page 269.**

GRAMMAR, USAGE, MECHANICS, SPELLING

Sentences

A **sentence** is a group of words that expresses a complete thought. Every sentence has two parts: a subject and a predicate.

Subjects

The **subject** is the part of a sentence that tells who or what is doing something. It can also name who or what is being talked about. In many sentences, the subject comes first and is followed by a predicate.

> My sister Cory loves horses.

> She is a fine rider.

★ **Simple Subject**

The **simple subject** is the main noun or pronoun in the complete subject.

> The gray horse ran into the barn.

★ **Complete Subject**

The **complete subject** includes the simple subject and all the words that tell about it.

> The gray horse ran into the barn.

★ **Compound Subject**

A **compound subject** is two or more subjects in a single sentence. The subjects are joined by *and* or *or*.

> Karen and my sisters are friends.

> Jane, Mark, or Jay will come.

Remember:
Every sentence needs a subject and a predicate to express a complete thought.

The **predicate** is the part of a sentence that tells what the subject is doing. It can also tell who or what the subject is.

Molly looked closely at her room.

The room seemed too old-fashioned to her.

★ **Simple Predicate**

The **simple predicate** is the main verb in the complete predicate.

Molly painted her bedroom.

She chose a bright shade of yellow.

★ **Complete Predicate**

The **complete predicate** includes the verb and all the words that describe it.

The paint brightened the room.

Molly rearranged her furniture.

★ **Compound Predicate**

A **compound predicate** is two or more predicates in a single sentence. The predicates are joined by *and* or *or*.

Molly made new curtains and hung them up.

She bought a colorful rug and put it on her floor.

> **Remember:**
> The predicate of a sentence tells what the subject is or does.

Sentence Structure

Sentences can vary, depending on their structure. These kinds of sentences include **simple, compound**, and **complex** sentences.

★ **Simple Sentences**

A **simple sentence** contains one complete thought. It may have more than one subject and more than one predicate.

> Jeff read the book.
>
> Jeff and Luis read the book.
>
> Jeff read the book and wrote a report.
>
> Luis read the book and created a diorama.

★ **Compound Sentences**

A **compound sentence** contains two or more simple sentences. The sentences are separated by a comma, and they can be joined by a connecting word such as *and, but,* or *or.*

> We finished our soup, and Mom gave us salad.
>
> I like salad, but I take out the tomatoes.
>
> I add cheddar cheese, or I sprinkle on some raisins.

★ **Complex Sentences**

A **complex sentence** has two closely related ideas. It contains one simple sentence and one or more incomplete sentences.

simple:	The streets were muddy.
incomplete:	After the storm ended
complex:	The streets were muddy after the storm ended.

simple:	We play soccer in the park.
incomplete:	When the weather is fair
complex:	We play soccer in the park when the weather is fair.

A **sentence fragment** is an incomplete sentence. It is missing a subject or a predicate. To correct a sentence fragment, simply add a subject or a predicate.

sentence fragment:	Our dog Reggie
corrected sentence:	Our dog Reggie sleeps on the sofa.
sentence fragment:	Chased the cat.
corrected sentence:	Reggie chased the cat.

Remember:

Be sure to write complete sentences to tell your ideas clearly.

Run-on Sentences

A **run-on sentence** is two or more complete sentences that are run together without punctuation or a joining word.

run-on sentence:	The dog barked the robbers ran away.
corrected sentence:	The dog barked, and the robbers ran away.

Combining and Expanding Sentences

Improve short, choppy sentences by combining two sentences to form one smoother sentence. A short sentence can also be expanded by adding details.

short sentences:	Dogs make good pets. Dogs are great companions.
combined sentence:	Dogs make good pets because they are great companions.
short sentence:	My dog likes music.
expanded sentence:	My dog likes music and will howl when I play certain songs.

Grammar and Usage

There are four basic types of sentences. Each type has a specific purpose.

★ **Declarative Sentences**

A **declarative sentence** is a statement. It ends with a period (.).

> The news is on at 11:00.
>
> I always listen for the weather report.

★ **Interrogative Sentences**

An **interrogative sentence** asks a question. It ends with a question mark (?).

> Is there a soccer game today?
>
> Which team will we play?

★ **Imperative Sentences**

An **imperative sentence** gives a command or makes a request. In some imperative sentences, the understood subject is *you*. An imperative sentence ends with a period (.).

> Listen to me.
>
> You listen to me.
>
> Fasten your seat belt in the car.

★ **Exclamatory Sentences**

An **exclamatory sentence** shows emotion, surprise, or strong feeling. It ends with an exclamation mark (!).

> I just saw a whale spouting!
>
> It was a huge humpback whale!

Remember:
Different types of sentences have different purposes.

A **noun** is a word that names a person, place, thing, or idea.

people	brother	coach	Jack
places	school	park	Canada
things	whale	canal	Dalmation
ideas	sadness	anger	hope

Common Nouns

A **common noun** is the general name of a person, place, thing, or idea. Common nouns are not capitalized.

sister   ocean   cat   love

Proper Nouns

A **proper noun** is the name of a specific person, place, or thing. Always capitalize proper nouns.

Sally Ride   Mount Everest   Golden Gate Bridge

Remember:
Begin each important word in a proper noun with a capital letter.

Singular and Plural Nouns

A **singular noun** names one person, place, thing, or idea. A **plural noun** names more than one person, place, thing, or idea.

The **plural forms** of most singular nouns are formed by adding *s*.

singular	teacher	park	movie
plural	teachers	parks	movies

Irregular Plural Nouns

Some **nouns** are irregular. You do not form their plurals by adding *s*.

★ **Nouns Ending in** *ss, sh, ch, x,* **or** *zz*
For singular nouns ending in *ss, sh, ch, x,* or *zz,* you form the plural by adding *es*.

> pass/passes   brush/brushes
>
> beach/beaches   fox/foxes   buzz/buzzes

★ **Nouns Ending in** *o*
For most singular nouns ending in *o*, add *s*.

> radio/radios   video/videos

For singular nouns ending in *o* after a consonant, add *es*.

> hero/heroes   tomato/tomatoes

★ **Nouns Ending in** *y*
For singular nouns ending in *y* following a consonant, change the *y* to *i* and add *es*.

> baby/babies   country/countries
>
> cry/cries

If the *y* comes after a vowel, do not change the *y* to *i*. Simply add *s*.

> key/keys   day/days   boy/boys

★ **Nouns With New Spellings**
Some nouns form a plural with a new spelling.

> ox/oxen   child/children   tooth/teeth

Other nouns have the same singular and plural form.

> salmon/salmon   deer/deer   elk/elk

A **possessive noun** shows that someone or something possesses, or owns, something else.

★ **Singular Nouns**

A **singular possessive noun** shows that someone or something owns something.

To form the possessive of a singular noun, add an apostrophe and *s*.

That is Maida's jacket.

The jacket's color is jade green.

When a singular noun ends with an *s* or a *z* sound, add both an apostrophe and *s*.

Tess's aunt is visiting from Mexico.

Gus's family is traveling to Europe.

Marcus's basketball team won the championship.

★ **Plural Nouns**

A **plural possessive noun** shows that two or more people or things own something.

To form the possessive of a plural noun that ends in *s*, add only an apostrophe.

My grandparents' car was damaged.

The boys' soccer game is today.

For a plural noun that does not end in *s*, add an apostrophe and *s*.

The children's pants were muddy.

The geese's feathers are wet.

The sheep's wool has been sheared.

Remember:

Most possessive nouns are formed by adding an apostrophe and an *s*.

Verbs

The **verb** is the main word in the predicate of a sentence. A verb expresses action or links the subject to another word in the sentence.

Action Verbs

An **action verb** tells what a subject does or did. Action verbs should be specific.

The hungry lion roared.

The frightened zebras flee across the grasslands.

The monkeys climbed the trees.

They quietly watch from a safe distance.

Helping Verbs

A **helping verb** comes before the main verb and helps the main verb state an action or show time.

Kimiko will jump over the hurdle.

Kimiko is jumping over the hurdle now.

Kimiko has jumped over the hurdle.

Did Kimiko jump over the hurdle?

Remember:
Use exact action verbs to make writing clear and vivid.

Common Helping Verbs

am	are	been	can
could	did	do	had
has	have	is	must
should	shall	will	would

A **linking verb** connects the subject of a sentence to a noun or an adjective in the predicate.

noun:	That team is the Redwings.
adjective:	The team seems unbeatable.
noun:	My hot dog is turkey.
adjective:	It tastes spicy.

★ **Forms of *be***

The forms of the verb *be* (*am, are, is, were, was, been*) are often linking verbs.

Donna was happy to play with her cats.

They were purring loudly.

★ **More Linking Verbs**

Other linking verbs tell what things are like or what they will become.

The roses smell sweet.

They look beautiful on the dining-room table.

Remember:

Linking verbs tell what things are like or what they will become.

More Linking Verbs			
appear	**become**	**feel**	**look**
seem	**smell**	**sound**	**taste**

Verb Tenses

The **verb tense** tells when the action of the verb takes place. The three common verb tenses are **present, past,** and **future.**

★ **Present Tense**

The **present tense** of a verb tells about an action that is happening now or one that happens regularly.

> The rain is leaking through the roof.
>
> The roof leaks all the time.

★ **Past Tense**

The **past tense** of a verb tells about an action that happened some time ago or over a period of time.

> The roof leaked in the ceiling of my bedroom.
>
> The roof had leaked for over a month.

★ **Future Tense**

The **future tense** of a verb tells about an action that will take place. The future tense is made by using the helping verb *will* before the main verb.

> The roof will leak again if it is not repaired.

Here are the **present**, **past**, and **future** tenses of some common verbs.

Present	Past	Future
arrive	arrived	will arrive
borrow	borrowed	will borrow
cover	covered	will cover
explain	explained	will explain
help	helped	will help
jump	jumped	will jump
laugh	laughed	will laugh

Most verbs are **regular verbs**. To tell about an action in the past, add *ed* or use a helping verb.

I paint. I painted. I have painted.

Some verbs are irregular. **Irregular verbs** do not add the ending *ed* to tell about an action in the past. You form the past tense of irregular verbs in special ways.

Present	Past	Past with *have, has,* or *had*
begin	began	begun
blow	blew	blown
break	broke	broken
bring	brought	brought
catch	caught	caught
come	came	come
draw	drew	drawn
drink	drank	drunk
eat	ate	eaten
fall	fell	fallen
find	found	found

Remember:
With most irregular verbs the word changes when you state an action in the past.

Grammar and Usage

More Irregular Verbs

Here are some more irregular verbs and their correct forms.

Present	Past	Past with *have, has,* or *had*
fly	flew	flown
give	gave	given
go	went	gone
grow	grew	grown
know	knew	known
ride	rode	ridden
ring	rang	rung
run	ran	run
say	said	said
see	saw	seen
shrink	shrank	shrunk
sing	sang	sung
swim	swam	swum
take	took	taken
throw	threw	thrown
write	wrote	written

Remember:
Some verbs are not regular. Use the chart for help when you form these verb tenses.

★ Subject-Verb Agreement

The subject and verb of a sentence must agree in number. If the subject is singular, make the verb singular by adding *s* or *es*.

> Ami plays hockey. She passes the puck to her partner.

For plural subjects, use plural verbs. They do not have an ending.

> Her friends play, too.

Some verbs sound similar but have different meanings. The following verbs are often misused. Check the list to make sure you are using the correct word.

★ may/can

May is used to ask permission or to express a possibility. *Can* shows that someone is able to do something.

> May I use the pen?
>
> I can lift that heavy bag.

★ let/leave

Let is a verb meaning "to allow." *Leave* means "to go away from" or "to let stay."

> Let me show you the way.
>
> Leave here now. Leave the radio on.

★ sit/sat/set

Sit means "to rest or stay in one place."
Sat is the past tense of *sit*. *Set* means "to put."

> Sit down and rest. I sat on a chair.
>
> Set the groceries on the counter.

★ doesn't/don't

Doesn't is a contraction meaning "does not."
Don't means "do not."

> I don't know how to play chess.
>
> My best friend doesn't know, either.

Remember:
You don't set on a chair, you sit on a chair.

Adjectives

An **adjective** is a word that describes a noun or pronoun.

The most common adjectives are general words that tell what kind or how many.

Heavy traffic jammed busy highways.

Some adjectives name particular persons, places, things, or ideas. Always capitalize these adjectives.

Max loves French food.

Adjectives usually come just before the noun that they describe. But sometimes they come after a linking verb such as *is* or *was*.

Our team is good.

Articles

The adjectives *a, an,* and *the* are called **articles.**

Did you see the muskrat?

I saw a furry animal.

I think it was an otter.

The article *a* is used before nouns that begin with a consonant. *An* is used before nouns that begin with a vowel.

Demonstrative Adjectives

Demonstrative adjectives point out or identify things that are nearby or far away.

use with nearby things:　this, these
use with faraway things:　that, those

Remember:
Never use the words *this here, these here,* or *that there* together!

The **comparative form** of an adjective shows how two people, places, things, or ideas are alike or different.

Add *er* to a one-syllable adjective and use the word *more* with most adjectives of two or more syllables.

> Jean is taller than her brother Matt.

> Matt is more sociable than Jean.

The **superlative form** of an adjective compares three or more people, places, things, or ideas.

Add *est* to one-syllable adjectives and use the word *most* with adjectives of two or more syllables.

> This band plays the greatest music.

> The drummer is the most popular band member.

Never add both *er* or *est* and the word *more* or *most* when you use adjectives to make a comparison.

> incorrect: Todd is more faster than Jason, but I am the most fastest on the team.

> correct: Todd is faster than Jason, but I am the fastest on the team.

Some adjectives use special words for the comparative and superlative forms.

Adjective	Comparative	Superlative
bad	worse	worst
few	less	least
good	better	best
many	more	most

Adverbs

An **adverb** is a word that describes a verb, an adjective, or another adverb. Most adverbs tell when, where, or how. Adverbs often end in *ly*.

when?	The air soon became hot.
where?	The volcano erupted nearby.
how?	Everyone quickly fled.

Comparative Adverbs

Like adjectives, adverbs can be used to compare. To form **comparative adverbs,** add *er* to one-syllable adverbs or use the words *more* or *less* with longer ones.

Rita climbs higher than her friends.

Rita climbs more often than her friends.

Rita seems less nervous than the others.

Superlative Adverbs

To form **superlative adverbs**, add *est* to one-syllable adverbs or use the words *most* or *least* with longer ones.

Rita climbed the highest distance for the day.

Rita climbs most often on Green Mountain.

Remember:

Don't use *er* and *most* together when you use an adverb to compare.

Negatives are words that mean "no." The adverbs *not, never, none, neither,* and *no* are negatives. Contractions with *not* are also negatives. Never use two negatives in the same part of a sentence.

incorrect:	I can't bake no more cookies.
correct:	I can't bake any more cookies.
incorrect:	There aren't no copies of the book left.
correct:	There aren't any copies of the book left.

Some adverbs have similar meanings. Check the list to make sure you're using them correctly.

★ **very/real**
Do not use *real* when you mean *very*.

incorrect:	It is real hot on that beach.
correct:	It is very hot on that beach.

★ **good/well**
Use *good* as an adjective. Use *well* as an adverb to mean "in a good way."

incorrect:	Maya studies good.
correct:	Maya studies well.
correct:	Maya is a good student.

Remember:

Never use *real* or *good* when you need an adverb.

Pronouns

A **pronoun** is a word that can replace a noun. Personal pronouns are words such as *I, you, me,* and *we.* Use them to refer to people.

Subject Pronouns

Use a **subject pronoun** to replace a noun in the subject of a sentence.

> Pia hit a home run. She tied the game.
>
> The fans cheered loudly.
>
> They think Pia is a great athlete.

Subject Pronouns			
singular	I	you	he, she, it
plural	we	you	they

Object Pronouns

Use an **object pronoun** to replace a noun that follows an action verb. Also use object pronouns after prepositions such as *at, about, for, from, in, into, of, near, through, to,* and *with.*

> Maggie's team cheered her.
>
> Will she hit another home run for us?

Object Pronouns			
singular	me	you	him, her, it
plural	us	you	them

Always use the word *I* as a subject pronoun. Use *me* as an object pronoun.

> I have a new tent.

> Marco gave Mark and me his tent.

> Marco saved it for us.

Possessive pronouns show ownership.

Possessive pronouns are usually used like adjectives to describe nouns.

> My trophy will look good in our room.

Possessive Pronouns With Nouns			
singular	**my**	**your**	**his, her, its**
plural	**our**	**your**	**their**

Some possessive pronouns are used by themselves.

> Is this book yours? No, it is mine.

Possessive Pronouns Alone			
singular	**mine**	**yours**	**his, hers**
plural	**ours**	**yours**	**theirs**

Remember:
Pronouns, like nouns, can show possession.

Interrogative Pronouns

Interrogative pronouns are usually used to ask questions.

Who will get the cake for the party?

Which of these sweaters should I wear?

What is that sound?

Interrogative Pronouns

who   whose   which   what

Pronoun Agreement

Pronouns should agree in number with the nouns they replace. Use singular pronouns to replace singular nouns. Use plural pronouns to replace plural nouns.

singular: The house looks terrific since it was painted.

plural: The other houses look as if they need paint, too.

Use the pronouns *he, him*, and *his* to refer to boys and men. Use *she, her*, and *hers* to refer to girls and women.

Allie plays guitar.

She is in a rock band.

Josh plays, too.

His guitar is brand-new.

Remember:

If a pronoun is the subject of a sentence, it must agree with the verb.

A **preposition** is a word that relates a noun or a pronoun to another word in a sentence.

> The astronauts landed on the moon.

Prepositions

Remember: Prepositions get you *off*, *under*, *on*, and *behind* things.

Common Prepositions

about	above	across	after	along	among
around	at	before	behind	below	beside
between	by	down	during	except	for
from	in	inside	into	like	near
of	off	on	out	outside	over
past	since	through	to	toward	until
under	up	upon	with	within	without

Prepositional Phrases

A **prepositional phrase** includes a preposition, the object of the preposition, and any describing words that come in between.

> The astronaut returned to the empty spacecraft.

A **conjunction** connects single words or groups of words in a sentence.

> The stray dog is hungry and cold.

> We can take him in or call the shelter.

Conjunctions

Coordinating conjunctions connect two or more words, phrases, or sentences.

> We can feed the dog, and we can give him a warm place to sleep.

Coordinating Conjunctions

and	but	for	nor	or	so	yet

Capitalization

Some words always begin with a capital letter. A capital letter signals a word of importance.

Names

Begin the **names** of people with a capital letter.

Ann Richards   Jonas Salk
Harriet Tubman   Ben Franklin

Pronoun *I*

Always write the **pronoun *I*** with a capital letter.

I thought I heard footsteps on the roof.
I laughed when I saw it was hail.

Initials

Capitalize the **initials** that stand for a person's name. Follow each initial with a period.

Linda M. Lopez   R. B. Taylor
J.F.K.   C. S. Lewis

Titles of People and Respect

Capitalize a title that is used with a person's name.

Dr. Pitlak   Ms. Leeds
Mayor Fogg   Governor Bush

Proper Nouns

Use a capital letter to begin a **proper noun** that names a specific person, place, thing, or idea.

Chief Joseph   Mars
Brooklyn Bridge   Stone Age

In the heading of a letter and in an envelope address, begin the names of streets, cities, and states with a capital letter.

address: 65 Crestview Street
            Brownsville, TX 75050

Use a capital letter to begin the first word in the greeting and in the closing of a letter.

greeting: Dear Velma,
closing: Sincerely yours,

Use a capital letter to begin the names of the days of the week, months of the year, and holidays.

Monday, September 7, is Labor Day.

Place names and geographical features are proper nouns. Begin the name of a specific place or geographical feature with a capital letter.

The Sears Tower is in Chicago, Illinois.

Mount Shasta is in the Cascade Range.

Remember:

Capitalize the names of the months but not the names of the seasons—summer, autumn, winter, and spring.

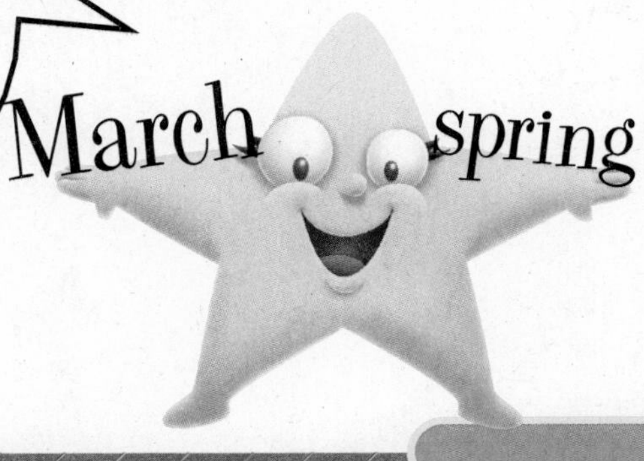

March spring

Nationalities and Languages

Capitalize the names of nationalities and languages.

Swazi   Irish

Spanish   English

First Word of a Sentence

Begin the first word of a sentence with a capital letter.

Where did you go on vacation?

We went to visit my grandmother.

She lives in Vermont.

First Word of a Direct Quotation

A direct quotation gives the speaker's own words. Begin the first word of a direct quotation with a capital letter.

Ben asked, "How many push-ups can you do?"

"Let's have a contest," I said. "Whoever does ten push-ups first is the winner."

If you are just reporting what you or someone else said, it is not a direct quotation. Do not begin with a capital letter.

Ben asked me how many push-ups I can do.

I said that we should have a contest.

Remember:

First words in a sentence or direct quotation should always be capitalized.

Writers often use outlines to plan their writing. Organize an outline into groups of main topics with subtopics. The main topic states the most important ideas. Subtopics add information and details that develop the main topics.

★ **When you make an outline,**
- capitalize the title.
- use Roman numerals such as I, II, and III to label the main topics.
- use a capital letter to label the subtopics.
- capitalize the first word of each subtopic.
- use a period after each Roman numeral and capital letter you use to label an outline part.

outline title:	The World of Dinosaurs
main topic:	I. Types of Dinosaurs
subtopic:	A. Plant-eating dinosaurs
details:	1. Apatosaurus
	2. Brachiosaurus
	B. Meat-eating dinosaurs
	1. Allosaurus
	2. Tyrannosaurus
	C. Birdlike dinosaurs
	1. Ichthyornis
	2. Pteranodon
	II. Reasons for extinction
	A. Climate
	B. Lack of food sources

Remember:

Each subtopic in an outline is indented and is labeled with a capital letter followed by a period.

Capitalization

Titles of Works

Works include books, magazines, songs, and movies. Begin the first, last, and all other important words in a title with a capital letter. Do not capitalize words like *the, an, in,* or *to* unless they are the first or last words.

book:	The View From Saturday
magazine:	Time for Kids
movie:	Treasure Island
song:	"This Land Is Your Land"

Headlines

A **headline** is the title of a newspaper article. Use a capital letter to begin the first, last, and all other important words in a headline. Do not capitalize words like *the, an, in,* or *to* unless they are the first or last words.

Student Wins Award for Art Project

Fourth Grade Visits Science Museum

Abbreviations

An **abbreviation** is a shortened form of a name, title, or some other word or phrase. Most abbreviations begin with a capital letter.

Mrs. L. L. Duncan is the manager.

U.S.A.F. stands for United States Air Force.

Is TX the abbreviation for Texas?

Common Abbreviations and Meanings			
a.m.	before noon	Mr.	mister
COD	cash on delivery	Mrs.	married woman
D.A.	district attorney	Ms.	title for a woman
Hwy.	highway	p.m.	after noon
M.D.	Doctor of Medicine	Rd.	road

Punctuation marks are special signals. Writers use them to make their meaning clear and understandable.

Punctuation

Indention

Writers signal the start of a paragraph by indenting the first line. Begin the first word approximately five spaces in from the left margin.

> Our school has bought new computers for the computer lab. The old ones will be put in classrooms. All the students are excited about this addition to our school. Now each student can spend time every day working on a computer.

Period

Writers use periods to signal the end of something. Here are some of the most important ways to use periods.

★ **To End Sentences**

Use a period at the end of sentences that make a statement or request.

> Our dog and cat are great pals.

> Bring that can of cat food to me.

★ **In Titles and Abbreviations**

Use a period after the short form of a person's title, after each initial of a person's name, and after some other abbreviated words.

> Last week, Dr. A. J. Iluta visited our class.

> common abbreviations: August/Aug.
> Street/St.
> Monday/Mon.
> Avenue/Ave.
> Lane/Ln.
> Road/Rd.
> Highway/Hwy.

Remember:

Use only one period to end a sentence when an abbreviation is the last word.

Question Mark

Use a question mark to end any sentence that asks a direct question.

What song will the band play for halftime**?**

Where did you buy your new CD**?**

When will you be able to go skating**?**

Sentences like the following do not ask direct questions. End those sentences with periods.

Mom asked whether I wanted more salad**.**

Dad wondered whether we would be able to go camping**.**

The ranger questioned us about feeding the bears**.**

Exclamation Point

An **exclamation** point is used to express strong feeling in a sentence. An exclamation point can be used after a word, a phrase, or at the end of a sentence.

a word:	Hey*!*
	Stop*!*
a phrase:	Happy holiday*!*
	Good luck*!*
end of a sentence:	Wow! Look at the lightning*!*
	Summer vacation begins today*!*

Remember:
Don't overuse exclamation points. They can make your writing shout.

Commas are used to keep words and ideas from running together in a sentence. Commas tell readers when to pause.

★ **In Dates and Addresses**

Use commas to set off the parts of dates and addresses. Use a period after the last item if it falls at the end of a sentence.

On July 20, 1969, humans landed on the moon.

We move to 5 Ames Street, Ogden, Utah, in May.

My new address is 787 Well Road, Austin, TX 78746.

★ **With City, State, and Country**

Use commas to separate the names of cities, states, or countries from the rest of the sentence when they are used together in sentences.

How far is Detroit, Michigan, from Quebec, Canada?

The streets of Venice, Italy, are canals.

We will move to Chicago, Illinois, this summer.

★ **In Letter Parts**

Use a comma after the **greeting** and **closing** of a friendly letter. For a business letter, use a comma after the closing, but use a colon after the greeting.

	Greeting	Closing
friendly letter	**Dear Aunt Maria,**	**Love,**
business letter	**Dear Judge Ortiz:**	**Sincerely,**

Ms. Maria Gonzalez
91 Cross Creek Rd.
Placitas, NM 87043

Remember:
Don't use a comma to separate the state from the ZIP code in an address.

Comma

★ **In Compound Sentences**

Use a comma before the coordinating conjunctions *and, but, or, nor, for, so,* and *yet* when these words are used to join two sentences. If the conjunction joins two sentence parts, do not use a comma.

two sentences: I must leave by noon, or I will be late for soccer practice.

two sentence parts: Should Dad or I bring a snack for the team?

★ **With Numbers**

Commas are used in numbers of four digits or more to keep the numbers clear and easy to read.

Light travels at 186,282 miles per second.

That used car costs $4,200.

Do not use a comma to separate numbers in years.

My grandfather was born in 1942.

★ **In a Series**

Use a comma to separate words, phrases, or clauses in a series.

Mr. Sung enjoys gardening, art, and poetry.

He grows orchids, makes pottery, and writes haiku poetry.

★ **After Introductory Words**

Use a comma after a word like *yes, no, hey,* or *wow* that begins a sentence.

Hey, wait for me!

Yes, I'll return tomorrow.

After Introductory Phrases

Use a comma to separate a long prepositional phrase from the rest of a sentence.

> In the morning before school, I jog with my dad.

> On days that Dad doesn't work late, we play basketball after dinner.

With Direct Quotations

★ Use a comma to separate the exact words of the speaker from the rest of the sentence.

> Jim shouted, "We need a home run."

With Direct Address

★ Use a comma to set off the name of a person being spoken to.

> Alana, be careful!

Remember:
No comma is needed when you report what a speaker has said. *Jim said that we should have won the game.*

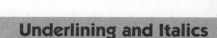

Underlining and Italics

Writers use **underlining** or **italics** (slanted type) to identify the titles of books, plays, movies, TV programs, and other long works. When you write such titles by hand, underline them. If you use a computer, you may be able to print italics.

> handwritten: I own a tape of <u>The Little Mermaid.</u>

> computer-printed: I own a tape of *The Little Mermaid.*

Apostrophe

An **apostrophe** is used to show that a letter or letters have been left out of a word. Apostrophes are also used to form plurals and show possession.

★ **In Contractions**

A **contraction** combines two words by leaving out one or more letters. An apostrophe replaces the missing letter or letters.

two words:	does not	you are
contraction:	doesn't	you're

★ **With Possessive Nouns**

Use an apostrophe before or after *s* to show possession. For more help with possessive nouns, see page 231.

singular noun: My dad's dream house is a log cabin.

singular noun
ending with *s*
or *z* sound: Tess's home is in the valley.

plural noun
ending in s: Two neighbors' houses are brick.

plural noun
not ending in s: The children's clubhouse is new.

Remember:

Add an apostrophe to the last name if possession is shared by more than one: *This is Tina, Josh, and Hannah's clubhouse.*

The KIDS' CLUB

Quotation marks are used to set off quotations and titles.

★ **Direct Quotations**

Use quotation marks around a speaker's exact words.

> Gina asked, "Is the school bus late?"

> "I think your watch is fast," said Robert.

★ **Titles**

Use quotation marks before and after titles of songs, poems, short stories, chapters of books, and articles from magazines and encyclopedias.

> "Hungry Mungry" is my favorite poem.

> Will you sing the verses of "America the Beautiful" for me?

Use a **colon** in a sentence to introduce a list of items. Use a colon instead of a comma after the greeting in a business letter.

> list: Here is what I need: a pen, a ruler, and paper.

> greeting: Dear Senator:

> **Remember:**
> When you use quotation marks or parentheses, add them before and after.

Parentheses are used to set apart words that give extra information or make an idea clearer in a sentence.

> The index (beginning on page 190) lists every name.

> The author used props (colorful puppets) to tell her story.

"before and after"

A **hyphen** is used to join or divide words. A hyphen is used to divide words into syllables, to make some compound words, and to form words that begin with prefixes like *great, all, self,* and *half.*

> bull's-eye great-grandparents self-help

Handwriting and Format

Neat handwriting and good penmanship are important to writers. If your handwriting is neat and clear, readers won't have to guess at words they can't make out. They'll be able to read your words with ease and concentrate on your ideas.

Handwriting

When you write a final draft of a letter, article, or story, be sure to write neatly and clearly. Here are letter forms you can use.

a b c d e f g h i j k l m n o
p q r s t u v w x y z
A B C D E F G H I J K L M
N O P Q R S T U V W X Y Z

Format

How your final copy looks is important, too.

Make it neat and clean. Keep your lines straight. Try not to make smudges or cross out too many words. If necessary, make a clean copy of your writing.

Use lined paper and keep equal margins. Leave one inch on the top, sides, and bottom of your paper. Sometimes, you may have to continue a story or report on a second page.

Write your name on every page. Use the heading your teacher tells you to use.

Remember:
Your paper represents you. Make it look its very best.

A Limerick
by Sean Kane

There once was a man named Lar
Who carefully studied the stars.
One night while in bed,
He saw something red.
Could this be the planet Mars?

As a writer, you have many great ideas to share. Misspelled words will make writing unclear to your readers. To make sure your words are spelled correctly, follow these spelling tips.

Use a dictionary to check the pronunciation of each word you are learning to spell. Knowing how to pronounce a word will help you remember how to spell it.

Dividing a word into syllables can help you spell a word. A word has as many syllables as it has vowel sounds.

Many words in English follow spelling patterns or rules. Knowing these rules will help you spell words correctly.

Syllables With Short Vowels

A **syllable** is a word or part of a word that has a single vowel sound. In words that have syllables with short vowel sounds, the vowel often comes between two consonants, following a consonant-vowel-consonant pattern. Knowing this pattern will help you spell words like these.

pencil   center   gentle

Syllables With Long Vowels

A long vowel has the same sound as its letter name. Knowing that many long vowel sounds are spelled with a consonant-vowel-consonant-final *e* pattern will help you spell words with syllables containing long vowel sounds like these.

alive   decide   outside   engage

Remember:
Learning basic spelling rules will help you avoid misspellings.

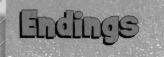

An **ending** is a letter or group of letters added at the end of a word. Writers add endings to make a word singular or plural or to tell when an action happened.

Words That End With a Consonant

Many words that end with a consonant do not need a spelling change before adding *s*, *ed*, or *ing*.

Word	s	ed	ing
melt	melts	melted	melting
print	prints	printed	printing

Words That End With *e*

If a word ends with a silent *e*, drop the *e* before adding *es*, *ed*, or *ing*.

Word	es	ed	ing
smile	smiles	smiled	smiling
skate	skates	skated	skating

Double the Final Consonant

Double the final consonant when adding *ed* or *ing* to a one-syllable word that ends with a single vowel plus a consonant.

Word	ed	ing
shop	shopped	shopping
grab	grabbed	grabbing

In one-syllable words that end with a consonant that follows two vowels, do not double the final consonant.

Word	ed	ing
shout	shouted	shouting
dream	dreamed	dreaming

Add *es* to verbs that end in *ss*, *sh*, *ch*, *x*, or *zz*. Do not change the spelling to add *ed* or *ing*.

Word	es	ed	ing
guess	guesses	guessed	guessing
smash	smashes	smashed	smashing
pitch	pitches	pitched	pitching

If a word ends with a consonant and *y*, change the *y* to *i* when you add the ending *es* or *ed*, but not *ing*.

Word	es	ed	ing
marry	marries	married	marrying
satisfy	satisfies	satisfied	satisfying

If a word ends in a vowel and *y*, just add the ending.

Word	s	ed	ing
obey	obeys	obeyed	obeying
enjoy	enjoys	enjoyed	enjoying

Remember:

Notice whether a word ends with a vowel + y or a consonant + y before you add an ending.

enjoy

Prefixes

Writers add prefixes to words to expand their choice of words. A **prefix** is a word part added to the beginning of a base word. A prefix forms a new word with a new meaning. Understanding the meanings of different prefixes will help you to use words correctly in your writing.

Do not change the spelling of a base word when you add a prefix.

prefix + base word = new word

pre + arrange = prearrange

This chart shows a list of common prefixes. Knowing the meaning of the prefix and base word will help you figure out the meaning of the new word.

Prefix	Meaning	Base Word	New Word
anti	against	freeze	antifreeze
ex	out	port	export
inter	between	national	international
micro	small	scope	microscope
non	not	fiction	nonfiction
pre	before	cook	precook
re	again	write	rewrite
sub	under, below	title	subtitle
un	not	realistic	unrealistic

Remember:

Pre means "before." Add a prefix before a base word.

Some prefixes mean "not" or "the opposite of." Knowing this will help you figure out the meaning of the new word.

Prefix	Meaning	Base Word	New Word
dis	not	agree	disagree
im	not	practical	impractical
in	not	correct	incorrect
non	not	sense	nonsense
un	not opposite of	happy	unhappy

Remember:

When you add a prefix to a word, don't change the spelling of the base word.

If you know the meaning of these number prefixes, you have a clue to the meaning of each word.

Prefix	Meaning	Base Word	New Word
mono	one	rail	monorail
uni	one	cycle	unicycle
bi	two	monthly	bimonthly
tri	three	angle	triangle

Suffixes

A **suffix** is a word part added at the end of a root, or base word. Knowing the meaning of a suffix will help you use the word correctly in your writing.

To add most suffixes, follow the same rules you use to add endings.

▶ **For help with adding endings, see pages 260–261.**

Suffix	Meaning	Base Word	New Word
able	able to be	repair	repairable
en	to make or become	short	shorten
er	one who	bake	baker
ful	full of	beauty	beautiful
ist	one who	art	artist
less	without	worth	worthless
ly	in a certain manner	live	lively
ness	state of	dark	darkness
ship	quality	friend	friendship
ion	state of	protect	protection

Schwa Sounds

The **schwa sound** is a vowel sound that is neither long nor short. Some words have a schwa-*l* sound or a schwa-*n* sound. These sounds can be spelled in different ways.

schwa-l: cable pencil tunnel local
schwa-n: women curtain lemon

A **root word**, or base word, is a word that is used as a base for forming other words. Word parts can be added at the beginning or end of a root.

cheer   cheerful   uncheerful

The spelling of the root word does not change when a prefix is added to make a new word.

▶ **For help with prefixes, see pages 262–263.**

re + order = reorder

dis + approve = disapprove

When adding a **suffix** or **ending** to a root word, you may need to change the spelling of the root.

▶ **For help with endings and suffixes, see pages 260–261 and 264.**

Rule	Example
No change	**protect + ing = protecting**
Keep silent e before a consonant	**sincere + ly = sincerely**
Drop silent e before a vowel	**leave + ing = leaving**
Change y to i	**beauty + ful = beautiful** **funny + est = funniest**
Double the final consonant in words ending with a vowel plus a consonant	**flat + en = flatten** **split + ing = splitting**

Remember:
Spelling changes are necessary when adding an ending or suffix to some root words.

Compound Words

A **compound word** is made of two or more words used together as a new word. There are three kinds of compound words. Use the dictionary to make sure you write each compound word correctly.

one-word compound:	bobsled	shoelace
two-word compound:	credit card	fishing rod
hyphenated compound:	send-off	bull's-eye

Homonyms

Homonyms are words that sound alike but have different spellings and meanings. The following are some examples of homonyms.

★ **bare/bear**

uncovered:	She covered her bare arms.
the animal:	A mother bear protects her cubs.

★ **board/bored**

wood:	Nail the board to the bench.
a feeling:	When Dad is bored, he builds things.

★ **capital/capitol**

main city:	Austin is the capital city of Texas.
a building:	My aunt works in the capitol building.

★ **cent/scent/sent**

money:	The toll is fifty cents.
smell:	The scent of lilacs is sweet.
past tense of *send*:	Grandma sent me a plane ticket.

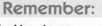

Remember:
Pick the homonym that fits the meaning of the sentence you are writing.

Here are more homonyms that cause writers special problems. Be sure to pick the spelling and meaning that fits what you mean to say.

★ **find/fined**

    locate: Did *you* find the library book?

    punished: I was fined for an overdue book.

★ **hair/hare**

    what's on *your* head: I wash *my* hair with baby shampoo.

    the animal: A hare has longer ears than a rabbit.

★ **heard/herd**

    listened: I heard an interesting folk tale.

    group of animals: The tale was about a herd of elephants.

★ **it's/its**

    contraction for *it is*:   It's still rainy.

    possessive pronoun: The tree has lost its leaves.

★ **they're/their/there**

    contraction for *they are*:   They're asleep.

    possessive pronoun: The dogs licked their paws.

    adverb "in that place":   We swim there.

★ **to/two/too**

    preposition: Bring that box to me.

    number: There are two boxes.

    "also":   Bring me that box, too.

    "very":   These boxes are too full

★ **who's/whose**

    contraction for *who is*:   Who's leaving with me?

    possessive pronoun: Whose coat is this?

Remember:

If you are not sure which homonym to use, check your dictionary.

Synonyms

Writers use **synonyms** and antonyms to help them find the right word. A synonym is a word that has the same or almost the same meaning as another word.

The building was quiet after hours.

It was so still I could hear my breathing.

Often a word has more than one synonym. Pick the one that best expresses your meaning.

The Indian elephant is a huge animal.

The extinct mastodon was mammoth!

But many dinosaurs were colossal!

Antonyms

An **antonym** is a word that is opposite or almost opposite in meaning to another word.

I was calm when I heard the news of our trip, but my sister was very excited.

Often a word has more than one antonym. Pick the one that best expresses your meaning.

The wrestler is thickset, but the dancer is slim.

The baby is chubby, but the model is slender.

A **thesaurus** can give you a choice of synonyms and antonyms for many words.

▶ **For help in using a thesaurus, see page 269.**

Remember:
Spice up your writing by choosing a synonym to replace overused words.

spicy

A **thesaurus** is a book of words and their synonyms. As a writer, you often need a more exact or interesting word. A thesaurus is a useful tool for finding just the right word.

Like a **dictionary,** a thesaurus has entry words listed in alphabetical order with a label showing the part of speech. A list of synonyms is given. The entry may also provide sample sentences and antonyms.

Thesaurus

entry word

part of speech

synonyms

graceful *adj.* adroit, agile, deft, nimble
These words share the meaning "having or showing skill, quickness, and ease in movement."
• My sister is a graceful dancer.
• An agile gymnast practiced on the trampoline.
• Thieves have deft hands.
• Pianists need nimble fingers.
antonym: awkward

definition

sample sentences

antonym

Use a thesaurus to revise your writing. If you are using a word-processing program with a computer in school or at home, you can use its Thesaurus function.

Remember:
When you use a thesaurus, try out different words in your sentence. Choose the one that sounds best and makes the most sense.

nutty
goofy
wacky
silly

Dictionary

A **dictionary** is one of a writer's best tools. Use a dictionary to define, pronounce, and spell new words you discover.

Entry Words

The words in a dictionary appear in alphabetical order. Each word that is defined is called an **entry word**.

Guide Words

At the top of every dictionary page is a pair of **guide words** that show the first word and last word on the page. Any word that comes between the guide words in alphabetical order can be found on the page.

Pronunciation Key

Each entry word in the dictionary has a respelling that shows how to pronounce the word. The **pronunciation key** lists the symbols used in the respellings. Each letter or symbol in the key stands for only one sound. This sound is shown in the word that follows the symbol, called the **key word**.

Division of Syllables

Both the **respelling** of an entry word and the **end line** show how to divide the word into syllables. In the respelling, spaces separate the syllables. In the end line, dots appear between syllables. The respelling also uses a dark stress mark (´) to tell which syllable is accented.

Parts of Speech

Dictionary entries tell a word's part of speech, using abbreviations such as **n.** (noun), **v.** (verb), **adj.** (adjective), **adv.** (adverb), among others.

A dictionary will list one or more definitions for each entry word. When a word has more than one meaning, the first meaning given is usually the most common.

guide words

squire ■ **stadium**

entry word

definitions

squire (skwīr) *n.* **1** a country gentleman who owns much land in England. **2** in earlier times, a young man who helped a knight.
squire ■ *n., plural* **squires**

squirm (skwurm) *v.* **1** to twist and turn the body as a snake does; wiggle *[The rabbit squirmed out of the trap.]* **2** to feel ashamed or embarrassed *[He squirmed when the teacher read his report.]*
squirm ■ *v.* **squirmed, squirming**

end line

pronunciation

squirrel

squirrel (skwur'əl) *n.* a small animal that lives in trees. It usually has a long, bushy tail.
squir·rel ■ *n., plural* **squirrels**

squirt (skwurt) *v.* **1** to shoot out in a thin stream; spurt. **2** to wet with liquid shot out in a thin stream *[Did you squirt the dog with the hose?]*
n. **1** the act of squirting. **2** a small, thin stream of liquid.
squirt ■ *v.* **squirted, squirting** ■ *n., plural* **squirts**

squirt gun *n.* a toy gun that shoots a stream of water.
squirt gun ■ *n., plural* **squirt guns**

squish (skwish) *v.* to make a soft, splashing sound when stepped on or squeezed *[The wet carpet squished under our feet.]*

parts of speech

squish ■ *v.* **squished, squishing**

Sr. *abbreviation for* senior *[Luis Montero, Sr.]*

Sri Lanka (srē läŋ'kə) a country on an island south of India. It was formerly called *Ceylon.*
Sri Lan·ka

St. *abbreviation for* **1** Saint *[St. Paul, Minnesota].* **2** Street *[42nd St.]*

stab (stab) *v.* **1** to pierce or wound with a knife or other pointed object *[She stabbed herself with a pencil.]* **2** to stick or drive a pointed object into something *[The farmer stabbed the pitchfork into the hay.]*
n. a thrust or a wound made with a pointed object.
—make a stab at or **take a stab at** to make an attempt at; to try *[Let's make a stab at fixing her bicycle.]*
stab ■ *v.* **stabbed, stabbing** ■ *n., plural* **stabs**

sample sentence

stability (stə bil'i tē) *n.* the condition of being stable or firm *[The stability of the government was threatened by the war.]*
sta·bil·i·ty

syllable division

stack (stak) *n.* **1** a large, neat pile of something such as straw or hay stored outdoors *[a haystack].* **2** a neat pile of something arranged in layers *[a stack of magazines].* **3** a chimney or smokestack.
v. to pile or arrange in a stack *[Stack your books.]*
stack ■ *n., plural* **stacks** ◄ *v.* **stacked, stacking**

plural

stadium (stā'dē əm) *n.* a place that is used for outdoor athletic events and other activities. It

718

a	cat	ō	go	ʉ	fur	ə = a *in* ago
ā	ape	ô	law, for	ch	chin	e *in* agent
ä	cot, car	oo	look	sh	she	i *in* pencil
e	ten	oo	tool	th	thin	o *in* atom
ē	me	oi	oil	th	then	u *in* circus
i	fit	ou	out	zh	measure	
ī	ice	u	up	ŋ	ring	

pronunciation key

Encyclopedia

An **encyclopedia** is a book or set of books that gives information about different subjects.

Each book, or volume, contains articles that are arranged in alphabetical order. Each book in a set of encyclopedias usually has a number on the spine and guide letters to let you know what topics will be found inside. Some encyclopedias are devoted to a single topic, such as science or plants or space.

The pages of an encyclopedia are like those of a dictionary, with guide words at the top of the page and entry words listed on the page.

The encyclopedia's entry words list the subjects or articles that can be found. Most articles begin with basic information. A list of related topics can be found at the end of the article.

entry word

article

Mount Saint Helens is a volcano in the Cascade Range, located 95 miles (153 kilometers) south of Seattle, Washington. After being dormant for 120 years, the volcano has erupted several times since 1980. The eruptions have caused hundreds of millions of dollars in damage. More than 1,000 feet (300 meters) of the mountain's peak was blasted away during the explosions, leaving a huge crater. The hot ashes and molten rock started forest fires and melted snow from the mountain, which in turn caused floods and mud slides, washing away buildings, roads, and bridges. Thick layers of volcanic ash destroyed crops and wildlife.

related topi

See also **Mountains.** (photograph)
Washington (picture): The eruptions of Mount St. Helens.

Use the Index volume of an encyclopedia to find more information about a topic. The index will tell you other areas to look at for information, pictures, photographs, diagrams, and related topics.

name of volume

page number

Volcano V: 367 with maps and photographs
    Crater *Ci:* 1098
    Earth *E:* 35
    Island (Volcanic Islands) *I:* 412
    Lava *L:* 144
    Mount Saint Helens *M:* 798
    Mountain (Volcanic Mountains) *M:* 867

related topics

Volume V: 368 with photographs

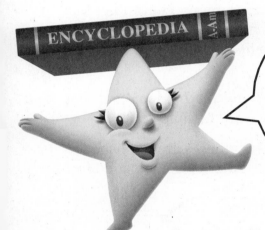

ENCYCLOPEDIA A–Am

Remember:
The Internet can connect you to other schools, libraries, museums, and people.

The **Internet** is also a popular source of information. You can find lots of great current information and download photographs and charts to make your writing more interesting.

Internet

To be sure you are getting accurate information, visit Web sites maintained by reliable organizations and companies. Your librarian or teacher can suggest several books that should lead you to good Web sites.

Some encyclopedias that are available on CD-ROM and the Internet present topics with the help of audio and video. You might hear a famous speech or watch a short movie of a news event in an encyclopedia with such features. Encyclopedias on the Internet are continually updated and provide links to related articles.

Atlas

An **atlas** is a book of maps. A complete world atlas also has information about climate, land formations, populations, cultures, and politics. If you use a map to learn information, it is important to know how to read it.

On many maps you will see a special symbol called a **compass rose**. This symbol is usually shaped like a cross, with an arrow pointing north. It helps you identify the directions north, south, east, and west on that map.

Each map has its own **legend,** or **key**. The legend, set in a box, explains other important symbols and marks on the map. Use the legend to understand how to recognize the symbols for cities, capital cities, boundaries, and names of states or countries.

One item in a map legend is the **map scale.** This scale shows the distance between places on that map. Scales differ from one map to another. On one map, 1 inch may represent 100 miles or just 1 mile. On another map, 1 centimeter may represent 500 kilometers. A map scale is a line that has been marked at set spaces, much like a ruler.

To determine the ground distance between two points on a map, measure the distance between them and compare that measurement to the distance on the map scale.

Like other reference resources, atlases are published as CD-ROMs for use with a computer or downloaded from the Internet.

Remember:
If you are trying to figure out a distance, start by looking at the map scale.

miles
0   5   10   15   20

0   6   12   18   24   30
kilometers

An **almanac** is a reference book filled with facts, figures, charts, and other information.

Almanacs are published every year and have information on dozens of subjects, from facts about foreign countries to lists of sports events. Because a new almanac is published each year, it is a good source of updated information on a wide range of topics.

Almanacs usually have facts and figures about these main topics.

> Important Events of the Previous Year
>
> Consumer Information
>
> Health
>
> Nations of the World
>
> People
>
> Religion
>
> Science and Technology
>
> Sports

A special almanac for kids might include records and facts about special topics.

> Amusement Centers
>
> Animals the World Over
>
> Computers and Videos
>
> Contests for Kids
>
> Inventions
>
> Museums
>
> Music

When you want to find information about a particular topic, always look in the index in the back of the almanac. This index will direct you to the correct page of the book.

Remember:

The information in an almanac will satisfy your curiosity as to *who, what, when, where,* and *how.*

Index

z

Art & Photo Credits

Illustrations: Front cover, pencilperson, starperson: Bernard Adnet. iii: *t.* Todd Nordling; *b.r.* Dee Deloy. iv: *t.* Dee Deloy; *b.r.* Jean Hirashima. v: *t.* Joy Allen; *m.l.* Bonnie Matthews; *b.* Doreen Gay Kassel. 2–3: Steve Gray. 5: Todd Nordling. 6, 9: Steve Gray. 10, 12, 15, 16: Todd Nordling. 18–19: Bernard Adnet. 20: Todd Nordling. 21, 22, 23, 24, 25, 26, 27, 29, 30–31, 32, 33: Dee Deloy. 38–39: Greg Newbold. 40: Douglas A. Bowles. 41: Bonnie Matthews. 42, 43: Andrea Wallace. 44–45: Douglas A. Bowles. 46, 47, 48: Jean Hirashima. 49: Bernard Adnet. 50–51: Joan Cottle. 52, 54: Delana Bettoli. 55, 56–57, 58, 59, 60, 61, 62–63, 64: Tom Pansini. 69, 70, 71, 72, 73, 74–75, 76, 77, 78: Lane Yerkes. 81, 82, 83: Melinda Levine. 85, 87, 88: Rosario Valderrama. 89: Bernard Adnet. 90–91: Bob Byrd. 92, 93, 94: Joy Allen. 95, 96, 97, 98, 99, 100, 102–103, 104, 105: Steve Henry. 106–107, 108, 109, 110: Lydia Taranovic. 111, 112– 113, 114, 115, 116–117, 118–119, 120, 121: Douglas A. Bowles. 122–123: Cheryl Kirk Noll. 124–125, 126: Brian White. 128–129: Gary Torrisi. 130, 131, 132, 133, 134: Bonnie Matthews. 135, 136, 138, 139, 140, 142, 143, 144: Jane Manning. 146–147, 148: Amy Wummer. 149, 150, 151, 153, 156, 158, 161, 162: Valerie Sokolova. 165, 166–167, 168: Amanda Haley. 169: Bernard Adnet. 170–171: C.D. Hullinger. 173: Tim Blough. 175, 176, 177, 179, 183: Diana Magnuson. 186, 187, 188, 189, 190: Don Petersen. 191, 192–193, 194, 195, 196–197, 200: Doreen Gay Kassel. 203, 204: Kelly Kennedy.

Photos: All photos ©Modern Curriculum Press unless otherwise noted.
v: *m.r.* Steve Ferry for Silver Burdett Ginn. vi: Jade Albert for Modern Curriculum Press. 4: Dorey A. Cardinale/Parker/Boone Productions for Modern Curriculum Press. 7: *r.* Courtesy of The Paper Company. 9: PhotoDisc, Inc. 32: *m.* ©John Serrao, The National Audubon Society Collection/Photo Researchers, Inc. 52: *t.* Every Living Thing Stories by Cynthia Rylant, Decorations by S.D. Schindler, Published by Bradbury Press/New York, ©1985; *b.* Simon & Schuster Children's Publishing Division. 66: Courtesy of United Features Syndicate. 67: Candy Courtesy of Sweethearts by Necco. 69, 70, 73, 78, 79: *t.* Steve Henry for Modern Curriculum Press. 80: Plays Children Love, Volume II, Edited by Coleman A. Jennings and Aurand Harris, Published by St. Martin's Press, ©1988. 87: Corbis–Bettmann. 92: *l.* Courtesy of Wayne Grover; *m.* Dolphin Adventure by Wayne Grover, Illustrated by Jim Fowler, Beech Tree Edition, 1993, originally published by Greenwillow Books. 95, 96, 104, 105: *t.* Greg Phelps/Phelps, Hollander, Millar for Modern Curriculum Press. 111, 112, 120, 121: *t.* Doug Wilson for Modern Curriculum Press. 122: *Flower Moon Snow, A Book of Haiku* by Kazue Mizumura, Illustrated with Woodcuts by the author, Published by Thomas Y. Crowell Company, ©1977. 124: *l.* Gretchen Tatge; *r. Go With the Poem, A New Collection Chosen by Lilian Moore,* Cover design by Kathleen Westray, Published by The McGraw–Hill Book Company, ©1977. 128: *r.* Anne Van Der Vaeren/The Image Bank. 129: PhotoDisc, Inc. 130: *t.* Sigrid Estrada; *b. Amber Brown Goes Fourth* by Paula Danziger, Illustrated by Tony Ross, Published by G.P. Putnam & Sons, ©1995. 135, 136 *t.,* 141, 144 *l.,* 145 *t.*: Michael Provost for Modern Curriculum Press. 149, 151, 153: Steve Ferry for Modern Curriculum Press. 154: *t.* Renne Stockdale/Animals Animals; *m.* PhotoDisc, Inc.; *b.* Zig Leszczynski/Animals Animals. 155: S. Michael Bisceglie/Animals Animals. 156: Steve Ferry for Modern Curriculum Press. 162: *t.* Paula Wright/Animals Animals; *m.t.* S. Michael Bisceglie/Animals Animals; *m.b.* Peter Weimann/Animals Animals; *b.* Steve Ferry for Modern Curriculum Press. 163: *t.* ©Alan Carey/Photo Researchers, Inc.; *m.r.* Steve Ferry for Modern Curriculum Press. 164: *l. Girl's Life* magazine. 172, 173, 174: Courtesy of U.S. Space Camp™. 175: Nancy Ferguson for Modern Curriculum Press. 178, 181: Utensils and Pots Courtesy of Sherri Hieber–Day. 184, 185: *t.* Nancy Ferguson for Modern Curriculum Press. 191, 195, 200, 201: *t.* Steve Ferry for Modern Curriculum Press. 216: Silver Burdett Ginn. 228: Jade Albert for Silver Burdett Ginn. 232: Silver Burdett Ginn. 236: Jade Albert for Silver Burdett Ginn. 240, 274: Silver Burdett Ginn.